JUNGL

to the Rescue

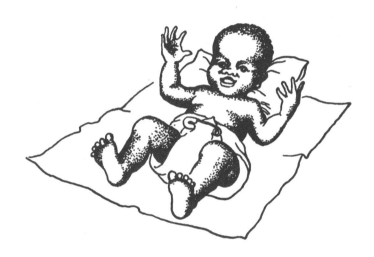

⑮

JUNGLE DOCTOR
to the Rescue

Paul White

CF4·K

10 9 8 7 6 5 4 3 2 1

Jungle Doctor to the Rescue ISBN 978-1-84550-516-5

© Copyright 1951 Paul White
First published 1951
Reprinted 1953, 1955, 1958, 1960, 1963, 1965
Paperback edition 1972
Published in 2009 by
Christian Focus Publications, Geanies House,
Fearn, Tain, Ross-shire, IV20 1TW, Scotland, U.K.
Fact files: © Copyright Christian Focus Publications
Paul White Productions,
4/1-5 Busaco Road, Marsfield, NSW 2122, Australia
Cover design: Daniel van Straaten
Cover illustration: Craig Howarth
Interior illustrations: Graham Wade
Printed and bound in Denmark by Norhaven A/S

Since the Jungle Doctor books were first published there have been a number of Jungle Doctors working in Mvumi Hospital, Tanzania, East Africa - some Australian, some British, a West Indian and a number of East African Jungle Doctors to name but a few.

Scripture quotations taken from the HOLY BIBLE, NEW INTERNATIONAL VERSION. Copyright © 1973, 1978, 1984 by International Bible Society. Used by permission of Hodder & Stoughton Publishers.

Some Scripture quotations are based on the King James Version of the Bible.

African words are used throughout the book, but explained at least once within the text. A glossary is also included at the front of the book along with a key character index.

CONTENTS

Fact File: Paul White

Born in 1910 in Bowral, New South Wales, Australia, Paul had Africa in his blood for as long as he could remember. His father captured his imagination with stories of his experiences in the Boer War which left an indelible impression. His father died of meningitis in army camp in 1915, and he was left an only child without his father at five years of age. He inherited his father's storytelling gift along with a mischievous sense of humour.

He committed his life to Christ as a sixteen-year-old schoolboy and studied medicine as the next step towards missionary work in Africa. Paul and his wife, Mary, left Sydney, with their small son, David, for Tanganyika in 1938. He always thought of this as his life's work but Mary's severe illness forced their early return to Sydney in 1941. Their daughter, Rosemary, was born while they were overseas.

Within weeks of landing in Sydney Paul was invited to begin a weekly radio broadcast which spread throughout Australia as the Jungle Doctor Broadcasts - the last of these was aired in 1985. The weekly scripts for these programmes became the raw material for the Jungle Doctor hospital stories - a series of twenty books.

Paul always said he preferred life to be a 'mixed grill' and so it was: writing, working as a Rheumatologist, public speaking, involvement with many Christian organisations, adapting the fable stories into multiple forms (comic books, audio cassettes, filmstrips), radio and television, and sharing his love of birds with others by producing bird song cassettes - and much more.

The books in part or whole have been translated into 107 languages.

Paul saw that although his plan to work in Africa for life was turned on its head, in God's better planning he was able to reach more people by coming home than by staying. It was a great joy to meet people over the years who told him they were on their way overseas to work in mission because of the books.

Paul's wife, Mary, died after a long illness in 1970. He married Ruth and they had the joy of working together on many new projects. He died in 1992 but the stories and fables continue to attract an enthusiastic readership of all ages.

Fact File: Tanzania

The *Jungle Doctor* books are based on Paul White's missionary experiences in Tanzania. Today many countries in Africa have gained their independence. This has resulted in a series of name changes. Tanganyika is one such country that has now changed its name to Tanzania.

The name Tanganyika is no longer used formally for the territory. Instead the name Tanganyika is used almost exclusively to mean the lake.

During World War I, what was then Tanganyika came under British military rule. On December 9, 1961 it became independent. In 1964, it joined with the island of Zanzibar to form the United Republic of Tanganyika and Zanzibar, changed later in the year to the United Republic of Tanzania.

It is not only its name that has changed, this area of Africa has gone through many changes since the Jungle Doctor books were first written. Africa itself has changed. Many of the same diseases raise their heads, but treatments have advanced. However new diseases come to take their place and the work goes on.

Missions throughout Africa are often now run by African Christians and not solely by foreign nationals. There are still the same problems to overcome however. The message of the gospel thankfully never changes and brings hope to those who listen and obey. The Jungle Doctor books are about this work to bring health and wellbeing to Africa as well as the good news of Jesus Christ and salvation.

Fact File: Pleurisy

Pleurisy is a term that you'll often hear people use when they have any acute chest problem. Medically, however, it means that the two membranes (called the pleura) that line the outside of the lungs and separate it from the chest wall are inflamed.

Pleurisy is often caused by a viral infection that actually affects the pleura. It may also be caused by something affecting an area of the lung, for example, pneumonia or a blood clot in the lung.

Anti-inflammatory medication will help to ease the symptoms by calming down the inflammation.

Fact File: Scabies

Scabies is a contagious skin condition that causes intense itching. It is caused by tiny mites called sarcoptes scabiei, which burrow into the skin. Scabies can be spread through close physical contact and, less commonly, through secondary contact with clothes and bed linen. Scabies is particularly widespread in countries that have a high population density and limited access to medical care.

Scabies is more common in children and women. Most outbreaks of scabies occur in winter, possibly because during this time of year people spend more time indoors and are in closer proximity to each other. Scabies can usually be successfully treated using special creams.

Crusted scabies can affect older people and people with certain illnesses that lower immunity, such as HIV.

Fact File: Malaria

In Africa, a child dies from malaria every thirty seconds. Malaria is an infectious disease that kills between one and three million people every year. Most of these deaths occur with young children in Sub-Saharan Africa.

When a mosquito bites, a small amount of blood is taken in which contains microscopic malaria parasites. These grow and mature in the mosquito's gut for a week or more, then travel to the salivary glands. When the mosquito next takes a blood meal, these parasites mix with the saliva and are injected into the bite.

The parasites grow and multiply in the liver and it can take as little as eight days or as long as several months before the parasites enter the red blood cells. After they mature, the infected red blood cells rupture, freeing the parasites to attack other red blood cells. Toxins released when the red cells burst cause the typical fever, chills, and flu-like malarial symptoms.

Malaria can be reduced by preventing mosquito bites with mosquito nets and insect repellents. Spraying insecticides inside houses and draining standing water where mosquitoes lay their eggs are two ways of controlling the disease.

No vaccine is currently available; preventative drugs must be taken continuously to reduce the risk of infection but these are often too expensive for people living in the third world. Malarial infections are treated through the use of drugs, such as quinine. However, drug resistance is increasingly common.

Fact File:Pneumonia

Pneumonia is inflammation of the tissues in one or both of your lungs. It's usually caused by an infection. At the end of the airways in your lungs there are clusters of tiny air sacs called alveoli.

If you have pneumonia, these tiny sacs become inflamed and fill up with fluid. As well as making you cough, the inflammation makes it harder for you to breathe. It also means your body is less able to absorb oxygen.

Pneumonia can affect people of any age. However, in some groups of people it's more common and can be more serious. For example:

• babies, young children and elderly people,
• people who smoke, and
• people with other health conditions, such as a lung condition or a lowered immune system.

People in these groups are also more likely to need treatment in hospital. Some forms of pneumonia can be more severe than others, depending on the cause. Mild pneumonia can usually be treated at home. People who are otherwise healthy usually recover well. However, complications can develop. For people with other health conditions, pneumonia can be severe and may need to be treated in hospital. Sometimes pneumonia can be fatal. It is possible to treat it with antibiotics such as penicillin.

Fact File: Words

WORDS TO ADD EXPRESSION AND EMPHASIS: Ah, Aha, Ahh, Eeeh, Eeh, Eh, Eh-heh, Heeee, Heeh, Heh, Ho, Hoh, Hongo, Huh, Kah, Ngheeh, Oooh, Salaam, Uh, Utye, Wah, Ya, Yeh, Yoh,

TANZANIAN LANGUAGES: Swahili (main language), Chigogo or Gogo (one of the 150 tribal languages)

SENTENCES/PHRASES:

Ale chaherera - We will get on our way

Assante - Thank you

Assante wose muno muno - Thank you everyone very much

Chi tayari - Tea is ready

Fundi kabisa - A very real expert

Hamba hadodo - Even a little bit

Hodi? – May I enter?

Hum nhawule - What's up now?

Kutula malaka - throat scraping

Mahala matitu - Of black wisdom

Mwana yungi - Another baby

Nani huyu - Who's that?

Nghani ya kwizina - A thing of wonder

Nyuma ya wachekulu - The women's ward

Nyumba ya afya ya wadodo - The room of health for babies

Sawa sawa - Exactly equal

Suma sana - It is poison

Swanu muno muno - Beautifully smooth

Tula malaka - Scrape teeth

Use mbera - You are wanted here quickly

Utamigweci - What's your complaint?

W'swanu du - All is well

Wataga mwana ayu, makatye yono yali manyagala nyagala, ninga yali mwana swanu - they threw out this child, they said he was just a nobody and rubbish, but he's beautiful.

Wusungu wuwaha - Great pain

Za henyu - What news of home?

WORDS IN ALPHABETICAL ORDER

Chaka - Without wisdom

Chetu - Customs

Chewi - Leopard

Chilili - Little bed

Cihulicizizo - stethoscope

Cizoka - Earthworm

Dudus – Insects/germs

Duka - Shop

Fundi - Expert

Heya - Yes/Amen

Ibolulu - Courtyard

Ihoma - Pneumonia

Ijego - Tooth

Ikuwo - Fierce anger

Izuguni - Mosquito

Karibu - Come in/welcome

Kaya - House

Kumbe - Behold!

Kweli - Truly

Lusona -Congratulations

Manghye - Doctor

Mbukwa - Good day

Mhungo - Malaria

Mimi -

Miti - Native medicine

Mitima - The soul

Mudala - Old woman who advises about babies

Muganga - Witchdoctor

Muhuzi - Gravy

Mukundugize - Push

Mulaguzi - Medicine man

Mulungu Umulungulungu - Almighty God

Mwanagu - My child

Mwili - The body

Ndege - Flutterings

Ndudududu - Sound of a bird

Ndudumizi - Little jungle bird

Nghangala - Mead

N'go - No

Nhembo - Elephant

Nhwiga - giraffe

Nyani - Monkey

Nzogolo - First cockcrow

Shauri - Discussion

Simba - Lion

Swanu - Good

Taka taka - Rubbish

Vipegwa - Money from 'curing' children with sore throats

Viswanu - All right

Wambereko - Childless ones

Warumi - Romans

Wubaga - Gruel

Wujimbi - Beer

Yayagwe - Help. O my mother!

Wadala - Native midwives

Warabu - Arabs

Wawambu - Slaves

Wugali - Porridge

Yakulema - He refuses

Fact File: Characters

Akisa - Teacher

Bwana - Dr White, main character/narrator

Bibi - Grandmother, term of respect

Daudi - Hospital manager

Dawa - Witchdoctor

Elizabeth - Patient

Majimbi - Wife of Lifuto

Mawinde - Baby's mother

Mwalimu - Teacher

Ndebeto - Baby's mother

Perisi - Wife of Simba, teacher

Sechelela - Head nurse

Sulimani - Indian

Elisha - Carpenter

Kefa - Nurse

Mamvula - Patient

Muganga - Witchdoctor

Mwendwa - Staff nurse

Nhoto - Majimbi's daughter

Raheli - Widow of Chamulomo

Simba - Lion hunter

Yohanna - Perisi's baby

1
Till the Teeth Come

'Three ounces less than last time.'

Perisi lifted the baby from the scales and put it into the African mother's arms. At the same time she picked up a blue pencil, steadily drew a down-going blue line on the child's weight-card and, looking up at the mother, who was swinging the baby on to her back, said:

'*Heh* – remember, no porridge until the teeth come.'

An old woman pushed forward. '*Hongo*,' she said in a wrathful voice, 'what do you know about it, you who have had no children?'

'*Ho*,' said Perisi, smiling all over her face, 'does one have to lay an egg to know whether it is a good one or a bad one?'

15

The old woman let flow a flood of words.

The African nurses who were sitting on the veranda near to me, mending surgical gloves, had a shocked expression on their faces.

The old woman shuffled off, laughing in a high-pitched cackle.

For a few moments there was one of those silences that you could almost feel; then one nurse said:

'*Huh*, those are the words of *mahala matitu*, of black wisdom; *huh*, it is an evil thing.'

Perisi went on unconcernedly weighing babies and marking up baby weight-cards. It was Tuesday afternoon at our hospital, and the day when baby welfare was the order of proceedings.

Mothers by the score had come; mothers whose infants had been born in the ward just across the way by the grove of frangipani trees; mothers who came for advice, for medicine; mothers who were attracted by the friendship and comradeship and the Christian influence of the C.M.S. Hospital at Mvumi in the Central Plains of Tanganyika.

The routine went on, babies were weighed, weight-cards marked, medicine handed out, and instructions given as to how to deal with this sore, or about the drops to be put into the babies' eyes or ears. Not once but a dozen times I heard: 'Now don't forget, only milk until the teeth appear. That is the way to keep the red marks going up and up on your card, and to make your baby stronger. That is the right way.'

It was quite late that same afternoon, and time to inspect that day's batch of babies.

'A quiet day, Bwana,' said Sechelela, the old African head nurse, 'four very ordinary babies. But then, of course, their mothers came to the hospital for many months to drink our medicine, and all these mothers know the ways of feeding a baby; they are all our people.'

'You know, Sech, it's so much easier when people will follow the ways of wisdom.'

'*Heh*,' said the old woman, 'but if someone came to you and said: "To eat bacon and eggs for breakfast is not a way of wisdom; to have a bath every day is bad for you; to wear shoes on your feet is not the right way to live," what would you say?'

'Perhaps, Sech, I would not agree with them, and then I would tell them that this is the way that I live.'

'Well, Bwana, don't you see that's what our women say when you come along? You say to them: "Come and drink the hospital's medicine," but they have never been used to doing that. You say to them: "Put the baby in a cot, don't leave him on the floor," but they have never been used to doing that. You say: "Give the baby no porridge to eat till he has teeth," but they say: "Did not my mother do that, and my grandmother, and my grandmother's grandmother? Why should I change our custom?" And you see, Bwana, you don't hear the stories that the people tell about you.'

'Tell me, Sech; what do they say? I would love to know.'

'Bwana,' said the old woman, driving home her points by tapping me with her forefinger on the shoulder, 'they say that in the hospital we break all the customs of the tribe. They tell stories of what you do that make their hearers shake with fright.'

'But, Sech, they can come and see what we do – everything is open for them to see.'

'Yes, Bwana, but they tell strange things, nonetheless. You put drops in the babies' eyes, and what do they say? "You pull out the baby's eye, draw it out long, squeeze it, and put it back again."'

'*Hongo*, Sech, that's absurd! It's silly; that's only an eye-dropper. Pull out a baby's eye and squeeze it! What rot!'

The old woman nodded her head.

'To you and to me, yes, Bwana; but what of the old women who used to make their money through helping the mothers? Is it not a good way to keep people from the hospital?'

'But are we not beginning to beat these evil old women and their weird stories? Surely more and more mothers are arriving each month and there seems no end to the number of babies being born here.'

Again she nodded. 'Are we not training women of the tribe to be nurses? Are we not gaining the confidence of the people themselves, and they are seeing that the new way is the better way?'

From inside the ward came the sound of singing.

'It's the Good News, Sech, that makes all the difference. Do you know that tune?'

The old woman nodded. 'It's "Tell me the old, old story of Jesus and His love."'

'Well, what we try to do here, you know, is to do the former and to show the latter.'

Sechelela nodded slowly. 'Bwana, all goes well these days here. Perisi works with good wisdom. But do not forget that in three short months she will be starting the new clinic at Makali.'

'I know it only too well. Simba, her husband, has been telling me a long story about all sorts of trouble he's going to meet; but I think he's only lonely without Perisi.'

Sechelela laughed. 'And who is there to cook his food while his wife is here dealing with babies?'

Suddenly, she was serious. '*Kah*, Bwana, and I, too, can feel within me that feeling of something that is going to happen' – she shivered – 'I had it before the famine, and before Bibi nearly died.'

I picked up my topee. '*Hongo*, Sech, cheer up, it is merely that you need some quinine; malaria is upon you.'

She shook her head and smiled wryly; together we went into the ward.

Perisi stood ready with the temperature book.

I bent over the first bed. '*Lusona!* Congratulations!'

The tired face of the mother smiled back at me.

'Lulo. Thank you, Bwana.' And then in a quiet voice: 'My seventh child, Bwana, and the only one born alive.'

'Eight-and-a-half pounds,' said the African nurse, in a matter of fact way. 'A boy with a powerful voice.'

'He's a great little chap; we'll help you to keep him well,' I said to the mother.

She smiled at her small son as he lay in his cot at the end of the bed.

I visited the eighteen beds in the ward, and the ten patients on the veranda, looking at babies, checking temperatures, or exchanging a few words with the folk.

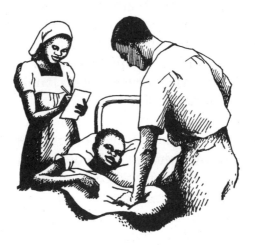

These means – simple advice and modern medicines – gave us the chance to save the lives of literally hundreds of babies.

One woman was swinging her child on to her back.

'Now, Mamvula, don't you give that child porridge till after the days of harvest.'

'*Yoh*?' said the woman, taken aback.

'*Heeee!*' said Perisi, behind me. 'Whoever saw a cow feed its calf on porridge?'

'Am I a cow?' replied the woman indignantly.

There was a gust of laughter from the women.

'No,' said Perisi, 'but at least have the wisdom of one!'

Coming to another group, my companion remarked:

'Milk's the thing. In milk is the vitamin, the small creature of great strength that doesn't live in porridge.'

'*Yoh!*' said one woman, 'is it a sort of caterpillar?'

'No,' smiled the African girl, 'it is not a *dudu*, an insect. It is strength. A baby full of milk is stronger than a baby full of porridge. See,' said she, pointing with her chin towards a married woman who swung her own child into view of everybody, 'milk, and no porridge. Look at hers.' She pointed with her chin to a woman carrying a six-months-old infant who was wasted, and utterly miserable-looking, 'That child was fed on porridge from its birth.'

At this moment a junior nurse came out.

'Bwana, Mamvula's baby is being very sick.'

I went back into the ward. The baby was being violently ill. Mentally, I saw a red light. This was the sort of case that, at home, sent you hot-foot for a specialist. But here, in Tanganyika, there was only one doctor, and he was specialist, builder, transport commission, post office, physician, police force, plumber and jack-of-all-trades.

I made a careful examination of the child and decided that the only thing to do was to wait for twenty-four hours and watch. At the end of twelve I was sure that I had to perform a major operation that I had never attempted before on a three-day-old baby. This surgical procedure was one of those finicky, dangerous sorts, when a slip meant death, and clumsiness might mean a life of ill-health.

After twenty-four hours I was certain that unless we operated, and did it quickly, there could be no hope. I sat in my office with a surgery manual before me, and checked over the operation, point by point. I had closed the book, when I heard a voice at the door.

'*Hodi*, Bwana?' There was the mother, wrapped in a sheet.

'Bwana, can you save him? *Yoh!* My heart is heavy. How I have longed for a living child, and now . . .' She put her head in her hands and wept.

I waited quietly until she was more composed. Then she looked up at the great book that I had reopened.

'Here,' I said, 'is a book that tells me how to help your child, how to relieve your baby of that thing that is killing him. See,' I pointed to a picture, 'it is as though he was being strangled inside.'

The mother nodded vaguely.

I reached over the surgery manual and pulled out a cheerful-looking little volume with a red cover. It was my hard-worked and well-worn Bible.

'Mamvula,' I said, 'this book I use more than the big one. It tells me how to get rid of the troubles of my soul, and of my spirit. It is the Word of God, and when you know the One who wrote it, you understand the meaning of His message to you. Listen!' I pointed to some words underlined. "So do not fear, for I am with you; do not be dismayed, for I am your God. I will strengthen you and help you; I will uphold you with my right hand."'

She nodded. 'So, Bwana, soon, when your knife and your iron tools are in your hand, you will know

that you are not alone, but you have strength.' She nodded upwards.

We knelt down, and very simply I prayed, asking God for strength and skill to save the life of that wee scrap of African humanity.

Now midday is not an ideal time to operate anywhere, but in the scorching heat of Central Tanganyika the theatre was almost unbearable.

The operation was halfway through; the vital stage was reached. I pointed to a thick, tough area.

'There,' I said, 'is the trouble.' And turning to the Australian nurse: 'Sister, if I cut an eighth of an inch too deeply, it is all up; and if I do not cut deeply enough, the operation is futile.'

I took up the knife. There was a hush. Two minutes later, with a sigh of relief, I looked at a job which I knew would go well.

But our troubles were not over. The African lad giving the anaesthetic said:

'Bwana, he is not breathing.'

With my mouth to his mouth, a gauze swab separating our lips, I breathed into his lungs. I suppose it was only a minute, but it seemed like an hour before the child coughed and started to breathe again. Hastily, I did all the sewing up necessary, and watched Perisi carry the baby back to the ward. Very quietly I said: 'Thank God, that's over,' and I meant it. I knew that I had not been working alone.

Daudi brought me back to the very day when he said:

'Bwana, your sewing is much better since you have begun to darn your own socks while you listen to the BBC news.'

I laughed, and putting on my topee went to the ward.

But trouble was still just around the corner. That evening, just after sunset, the child collapsed. A blood transfusion had to be given. The preliminaries were fixed up at an amazing rate – for Africa – and by the light of the hurricane lantern I watched the mother's blood run into the veins of her child. The little fellow responded almost at once.

Mamvula bent over him: 'Bwana, I'd give my life for this child.'

I nodded. 'Yes, I can see that.' And then, as I cut a square of sticking plaster: 'Mamvula, do you realize that God loves you like that? That He gave His life and died a criminal's death, to pay the price of your wrongdoing?'

She nodded her head. 'I am understanding it now, Bwana.'

She put out her hand and stroked the baby's arm. 'I think I understand it more clearly than ever, after today.'

Perisi looked at me and smiled.

2

One Tooth Less

'Daudi, what are four hundred and thirty-two and three hundred and twenty-nine?'

'Seven hundred and sixty-one, Bwana.'

'*Heh*, how did you get that done so quickly? I'm afraid I would have had to write it down and work it out on my fingers.'

The African dispenser laughed. 'Bwana, that's just what I did five minutes before you came in! Anyway, seven hundred and sixty-one is a pretty good total when you think that you and Bibi have all the work to do in the maternity ward.'

'Seven hundred and sixty-one – that's just about two babies a day.'

'Or a night, Bwana,' said Daudi, grinning.

Many a night he had seen my hurricane lantern moving along that quarter-of-a-mile which separated my house from the hospital.'

'It has been a most successful year. We have saved hundreds of babies' lives at two shillings a time. Back in my home country two shillings would not buy much, but over here it means that we save a baby's life.'

'Bwana,' said the African, 'I never thought of it like that. You know, my mother had ten children, but when the *mudala*, the old woman who advised about babies, and the *muganga*, the witchdoctor, and the *mulaguzi*, the man who made special medicines, when they all had finished, *kumbe!* My mother had only two children left.'

The African shook his head and went on: 'I was only small, but I remember hearing her crying at night and wailing the way that African mothers do because of the death of her children. Even though I was small I thought it was very sad, but now I can see that it was so unnecessary. With our baby clinic and our maternity ward, our vitamin oils and the baby weight-cards, the Baby Weeks and all the other things that we do, *heh*, we save mothers from very, very much sorrow.'

'Not only that, Daudi, but we manage to get the children along to hospital. They get malaria, and we can make them better with quinine. They get tick fever and we make them better with bismuth injections. They get pneumonia and we give them penicillin.'

'*Kweli*, truly, Bwana. Our hospitals are very useful, but don't forget we cause much anger to grow in the hearts of the witch doctors, and most of all to the *wadala*, the old women whose work it is to bring the children into the world. Have we not taken their livelihoods from them? They have fought us in many ways. They whispered that the C.M.S. nurse would blind the babies. They said: "What should a man, a mere man, know about how a child should be looked after!" I have seen them, Bwana, wave their hands around and use very strong words and spit in disgust when they mentioned you.'

'Let them spit, Daudi; as long as we do the job and keep on gaining the confidence of the people, I don't mind what they say.'

'But, Bwana, perhaps the time will come when they will do more than talk. They will perhaps act.'

'What do you mean? Stab me, or try to poison my food, or anything interesting like that?'

'They might do that, Bwana, but more likely they will drive nails into our tanks, steal hospital sheets, try to stop people from letting their children come to the hospital to train as nurses and dispensers.'

'*Hodi*?' came a voice at the door.

'*Karibu*,' I replied, 'Come in.'

'Bwana,' said a junior dispenser, 'have you forgotten? Today is the day for teeth. I have seven men sitting out under a thorn tree washing out their mouths with permanganate.'

I looked through the window at a strange scene. A petrol box and an ordinary form were the furnishings of this jungle dental clinic. Seven Africans were industriously washing out their mouths and ejecting the purple fluid expertly. Every now and then one would hold out his mug for more of the purple fluid and was given it by a small boy who was convalescing from severe malaria. In the shade of the thorn tree was Kefa with the primus going and a kerosene-tin steriliser on top. I walked over and examined the teeth. A dish, soap, and nail-brush were provided. I took off my coat, hung it on a convenient limb of a thornbush,

pushed my topee back on my head, walked over, and selecting an appropriate forceps proceeded to remove teeth.

The small boy filled up the mug of the first victim with the purple solution. His mouth was not a picture. His teeth could have been removed easily with bare hands if I had had enough courage. I scrubbed my hands, selected further forceps and dealt with my next patient.

In half-an-hour my dental job was over. My patients had been regaled with aspirin and a cup of tea and everybody was happy. As I watched them walk home along the various paths that radiated out from the hill on which our C.M.S. Hospital was built, clutching firmly in their hands the products of my handiwork, I felt that everything was going smoothly, and that we had had a good year.

I was perched on the ridge of the roof of the Children's Ward, busy with the not very medical task of soldering up holes in corrugated iron. Below me, sitting under the rather straggly pomegranate tree which existed in our hospital grounds, was a young woman apparently laying down the law, if the way she wagged her finger was any indication, to an old woman who sat there with her head in her hands. Even in the distance I could hear 'Wah . . .' Suddenly she stopped her noises, opened her mouth wide and pointed dramatically to a back tooth. Her companion stooped down to peer interestedly at the cause of the trouble.

Daudi hurried up the ladder with a fresh red-hot soldering iron. For a moment I concentrated on the none too easy job before me, then I said:

'Who are those two folk over there, the old woman making all the noise, and the girl beside her?'

'*Hongo*, Bwana, she is the old woman who cursed you and spat with vigour the other day.' She turned, and I recognized her at once. 'Bwana,' Daudi went on, 'those are people of trouble. The old woman is Majimbi. She is one of those who fills her grain bin from the *vipegwa*, the money that she gets from curing . . .' – at that word he turned up his nose in fine contempt – 'curing, Bwana, children whose throats are sore. *Yah*, does she not sharpen up the finger nails of these fingers?' He held up his first and second fingers and sharpened them on an imaginary piece of sandstone. 'She tells the people that all the trouble that the child has comes from teeth, strange and evil teeth, that grow in the back of the throat. These she has special skill in removing. So with her sharpened finger nails she scrapes the back of the child's throat, removing them. They call this *Kutula Malaka*.'

'If anyone tried to do that to me, Daudi, I'd bite them.'

'*Heeh, heh*, Bwana, perhaps you'd try; but old Majimbi, she pinches the child's cheek in between his teeth, so that if he bites, he bites himself, and then she claws away at the back of his throat. Truly, many children have died because of that old hag.'

'Well, she's not a very nice sort of person to have round the place. Who is the girl with her?'

'Bwana, that is her daughter, Nhoto. She is one of the wives of the chief of Lifuto. Behold, has he not sent her to the hospital, for does he not desire an heir? Four of her children have died even before their teeth appeared, and so he has sent her to us. *Yah,* Bwana, she and her mother are people of trouble. We must watch them.'

Even as he spoke the two got up and walked over to where we were working.

'Bwana,' said the old woman in a high pitched voice, 'Bwana, I have great pain in my tooth. This one' . . . with a long bony finger she pointed to her upper jaw. 'Give me medicine for it.' She peered at me in a way that seemed to question whether I would recognize her. I gave no sign of doing this, but climbed down the ladder and turned her old wrinkled head until the bright light of the sun shone right on her horrible collection of yellow teeth. The gums seemed to have shrunk back in disgust from them. Unless I had been fairly quick she would have taken my finger and pushed it back in her mouth to indicate the tooth in question.

It was obvious that old Sechelela had been bathing babies. She had one in her arms as she came across to where we stood, her chin pointing aggressively towards the old African woman.

'*Yah*,' she said, 'do you come to the Bwana and ask him to remove your tooth when you are in trouble?

You curse him one day and you seek his help the next. *Kah*, and are you not a *fundi*, an expert? You who remove teeth from other people's throats, can you not remove your own?'

Majimbi's voice took on a whining note. '*Hongo*, Bwana, don't take any notice of her words. Help me, Bwana; the pain, *heeh! Yah!* The pain.'

'*Kah*,' said Sechelela, wagging her finger, 'and behold, what of the children whose lives you have ended because of your evil ways?'

'Bwana,' said the woman, 'have pity on an old woman who has pain in her face. Do not listen to the words of Sechelela.'

'Of course I will help,' I answered. The old woman smirked and gave Sechelela a look of triumph. The African nurse caught a gleam in my eye and said nothing.

'Come into the sun,' I ordered, picking up a small mirror and a thin slither of wood. A stool was brought, and I swivelled my patient round, till the sun shone over my shoulder. With the mirror I flashed the light into her mouth.

Firmly I pushed down her tongue, which rebelled strongly again my wooden depressor. '*Utye Ahhh!* – Say *Ahhh!*' I urged her.

She spluttered and tried to talk, but the depressor was firmly held in place, and Daudi held her head just as firmly.

'*Ahhh!*' I urged, 'say *Ahhh!*'

'*Ahhh!*' gulped Majimbi.

'*Yoh*,' I said with enthusiasm. 'Look, Sech, she has teeth in her throat – I shall need to *tula malaka* and scrape them out.'

A look of absolute terror came into the woman's eyes. She dragged her head away.

'*Kah*,' she gasped, 'you shall not do that *hamba hadodo*, even a little bit.'

'What?' I asked, 'you who know so well the value of this treatment, do you refuse it?' She gulped but said nothing.

'Is it that you do not think your medicine is worth having?' taunted Sechelela.

'*Kah*,' snarled Majimbi, '*Nyamale twi*, shut up!'

'*Yoh!*' I spoke sternly. 'That is no way to talk. Do you or don't you want my help?'

'Bwana,' whined the old woman, 'remove this tooth, it is this one.' She prodded with a filthy finger at the obviously offending malefactor.

Daudi had boiled up the instruments. I scrubbed my hands and picked up the dental syringe, but Majimbi screamed, and ran away, followed by a burst of laughter.

A quarter-of-an-hour later she clasped the tooth in a piece of cotton wool and washed out her mouth noisily with a pink solution of permanganate.

'*Assante*, Bwana,' she said. 'Surely you are a *fundi kabisa*, a very real expert.'

'Majimbi,' again I spoke severely, 'mend your ways, give up the ways of bad medicine.'

'*Heee*, Bwana, I will,' she nodded.

Sechelela lifted up her eyebrows, smiled a very knowing smile and whispered into my ear: 'The zebra will also lose his stripes, and the *chewi*, the leopard, his spots.'

She called me into the store, it seemed for the purpose of opening a kerosene tin; but after closing the door she turned to me with a very serious face and said: 'Bwana, those are people of trouble. I have heard many words these days, and they are words of truth.

'At the well Majimbi has had bold words in the ears of the women. Did she not say: "Perisi, the wife of Simba, leaves the tribal ways to speak the tongue of the Wazungu, and follow their words."' Akisa the teacher heard her words and said: "These days, when the women find the better way of the hospital, and the wisdom of Perisi, is there not a famine in the houses of the *wadala*?"

'*Kumbe*, Bwana, Majimbi had fierce anger and said: "Shall this Perisi have children of her own, medicine shall be upon her path and she shall have the shame of the *wambereko*, the childless ones. She shall also hear the laughter of the *wadala* and have the great sadness."'

'*Kah*, Sech,' I said. 'Words, nothing but words.'

She shook her head. '*Hongo*, will you not understand that these things are a more real pain and fear in the heart of a girl than was that tooth in the jaw of Majimbi, the most evil of the *wadala*?'

We stepped out on the veranda again and watched the old woman and her daughter pick up their cooking-pots and walk out through the gate into the mellow colouring of the African sunset.

As I walked to my house that evening I was feeling that we had been very wise in planting crops in our hospital grounds. I thought of the twenty bags full of peanuts which would be a most useful source of food for our staff in the long dry season that lay ahead.

In bed I lay for a while listening to the howl of a hyena, the yelping of jackals and the persistent buzz of mosquitoes. But I was not left in peace for long.

About midnight I was called with the inevitable: 'Bwana, come quickly, *mwana yunji* – another baby.' Two hours later I was again between sheets. Silhouetted against the night sky was a tame lizard which crawled up the wire gauze and dealt effectively with mosquitoes and other *dudus*. Meditating on the jungle noises, I drowsed off, and it seemed only minutes later that I awoke with a start, one of those sickening awakenings when you are dragged from deep sleep to full wakefulness in a second. A voice was screaming outside:

'Bwana, Bwana, help, witchcraft, black magic.'

I leaped out of bed to see a dull glow in the sky. Then I heard another voice:

'Bwana, the store is on fire.'

In a twinkling I was sufficiently dressed and racing to the hospital. Everybody was in a state of panic, and had done nothing. I rushed to the tank, turned on the tap, but no water came. A great patch of moist earth on one side told a mute story of what had happened. I ran round, this time with four dressers behind me, each armed with a bucket, to the concrete tank outside the ward. We filled our buckets and rushed back to the fire, throwing the water at the seat of the flames. Soon everyone was following our example, nurses, and even small children with gourds, tins, anything that would hold water. The flames were soon under control and mercifully had not spread to the hospital buildings. The grass roof of the store had burned like tinder and the contents were smouldering ashes. My bags of peanuts, weeks of hard work, had gone up in a quarter-of-an-hour. Against one wall was a blackened kerosene tin, its side gashed by a native axe. I went to the store to check the number of tins there. Sure enough one had gone, and I remembered the empty tank. Somebody had been up to dirty work. Then I noticed Daudi's absence.

'Where's Daudi?' I asked. 'I know he sleeps like one dead, but the noise tonight was enough to waken even him.'

No one had seen him; no one knew where he was, and dawn was just breaking. My cook-boy, wakened by the uproar, had arrived on the scene with an enormous teapot, suitably charged. We were sitting around drinking, myself in silence, the others in a variety of keys! A weary-looking figure walked in through the gate and sank down on a three-legged stool. It was Daudi.

'Where have you been?' I asked.

He spoke in English. 'Bwana, I have been the policeman. When the fire started I saw someone rush past my window. I followed, down the hill, past the gardens. There it was they disappeared, but beyond the lake, near to the hill of the leopard, I saw in the

35

moonlight one of the *wadala* who used to look after the arrival of the babies – one of those who continually say evil things about our hospital. She was sitting before her house surrounded by those of her kind. I could not hear their words, but suddenly she threw up her hands and laughed, that cracked laugh we have heard before. Bwana, this is a bad business.'

I nodded in agreement. 'But I'm only thankful, Daudi, that it didn't occur before we set out on our three-day safari.'

3

Hostility Bristles

When Daudi and I went on a medical safari we would stop a whole day at a village, see all the sick people there, perhaps do a minor operation or two and renew the acquaintance of a number of our old friends. There would be those who would rub happily the place where they had received attention. Others would show the spot where tropical ulcers had been healed. Others

again would show a gap in their generally splendid teeth where one had given way and I had applied the gentle dental art.

I enjoyed these safaris. We used to sleep in the back of the car with a mosquito net as a rather inadequate boundary wall between us and the jungle. On this particular occasion we planned to spend a day with Simba at Makali, taking Perisi to see the progress he was making with the building of her new home.

We said the usual farewells as we drove away from the gates of the hospital, and by mid-morning we had reached our first village, greeted the Chief, seen a score of sick people, and arranged for Perisi to visit some of her former school-fellows.

The afternoon saw an ever increasing collection of Africans wanting medicine, injections, eye-drops and all the things that in an increasing way were being recognized as 'the new road to health,' as the Chief expressed it in his invitation to an evening meal of African porridge.

Round the campfire we listened to the stories of the tribe – how the rabbit outwitted the crow, and how the little jungle bird, *ndudumizi*, had overcome Simba, the lion, the king of the forest.

During a pause in the conversation I looked out into the cold, clear starlight and saw the silhouette of great palm trees, and behind them the green masses of a mango grove.

'*Kah*,' I said, 'behold, the *warabu*, the Arabs, have been here at one stage.'

'*Heeh*, Bwana,' nodded the Chief, 'this was a place where there were many *wawambu*, slaves. It was a place of grief before the British came here.'

'*Kah*, tell me this. If a man was caught by the slave traders, how could he be made free again?'

'*Heh*,' said the Chief. 'Bwana, it would cost much money for him to be brought back.'

'Listen, great ones,' I said. 'Listen to these words before you go to your rest. These are not my words, they are those of *Mulungu Umulungulungu*, the Almighty God, writing to you and to me. They are His words: "You were not bought back from the slavery of sin by things that can wear out, like money, but you were bought back by the precious blood of Christ!"'

Then I told them how the Son of God had died to pay the price for us to be redeemed, bought back, to freedom.

'But, Bwana,' asked one of the younger men whom I recognized as having had quite a reasonable education, 'does God demand the blood of His own Son before He will forgive you and me?'

'*Uh, uh*,' I said, shaking my head, 'you have it wrong. He is a loving God who tries to make us understand what a foul thing sin is. Did not Jesus Himself tell the story? There was a great chief, who, of course, was God in this story. He had a very big garden in which he planted many fruit trees and vines. He put a very strong *ibolulu*, fence, round it, and then it had a well, a house, and a place to store his food. So He sent men to look after His garden, and when the time came for the fruit to ripen He sent a servant and said: "Bring me of the fruit of My garden." But the men who looked after the garden took the servant and threw him out.'

'*Yah*,' said the Chief, 'I would have made trouble if that was done to one of my men.'

I nodded. 'The Chief was unhappy. He sent another, and this messenger came and said the Chief would taste of the fruit of His garden. But, before he could say more they attacked him with spears, and clubs, and treated him very shamefully.'

'*Yah*,' said the Chief. 'Now is the time for those men to be taught a lesson.'

'*Heeh*,' I said, 'but behold, the Chief with great patience sent other messengers. Some of them they beat, others they drove out of the place, and some they killed. But in the end, the Chief said: "How can I make these gardeners understand?" So He said: "I will send My only Son. When they see Him, they will know that He comes from Me, as if I were to come Myself; then they will understand."

'But these gardeners – every one of them – when they saw the Chief's Son come, said: "*Heh*, here he comes, the only Son of the Chief. Behold, we will kill him and then the garden will be ours."'

'*Kah*,' said the Chief, 'those men should be destroyed, Bwana. They were very evil.'

I turned to the African lad who had spoken. 'Behold,' I said, 'there is a picture of God's love. Chance after chance was given to man, but to underline what God thinks about sin, He sent His only Son willingly to die, to show us the danger of sin, to drive it home to us, not with wrath, but with love, that we should not forget. But listen, if we do not follow the way of life and love, make no mistake, the anger of Almighty God awaits the people who do not take the pathway of love that He prepares.'

That night as I lay curled up in my blankets in the back of the car, I thought of the tremendous need of these people who seemed to have no one to help them but us and our hospital.

At crack of dawn we were on our way again. Ahead of us loomed the village of Makali.

'*Heh*, Daudi,' I said, 'this is Simba's village.'

Our reception was a very real contrast to that of the night before. Hardly anyone had come for medicine. From some small boys I learned that there was much sickness in the village, but they ran away when they saw some of the elders of the place walk past without even the customary greetings. There was an air of bristling hostility.

That evening I was sitting outside Simba's partly-finished house and drinking tea prepared by Perisi.

'*Kumbe*, Bwana,' said Simba, 'there is trouble here. Behold, last night the Chief died, for he had only the medicine of the witchdoctor, Dawa, who is his relative. And now, Bwana, behold, they say in your coming you have cast a spell because you were jealous of the other witchdoctor. Behold, Bwana, I fear there will be trouble.'

I turned to my dispenser. 'Do you know this Dawa chap, Daudi?'

'*Kah*,' he said, 'Bwana, indeed I do. He lives in the hills right over there.' He pointed with his chin. 'Behold, he makes much wealth in fees of cows and sheep, gourds full of millet, and in shillings too. People pay very highly for the charms that he makes, and the medicines he produces. *Kah*, Bwana, some of them are foul. *Hongo*, Bwana, and do they pay for his witchcraft? – he talks with spirits, and with the devil himself. *Yah*, Bwana, very strange things happen there.'

'Make no mistake about it, Daudi, people who work with the devil do strange things all right. There is never a time when the devil is not fighting against the work of God, and if he can get men who will be on his side, *kumbe*, he gets them. The matter is very weird and very unnatural.'

This time Daudi shivered; but, as if to bring us back to earth, from not far behind the corn-cob shelter where we were sitting round the fire came the strident braying of a donkey.

'Bwana,' said Perisi, speaking for the first time, 'this Dawa is a small man, but he has eyes that seem to bore into you. When he commands, men obey. *Heeh*, and he walks around like a man who is conscious of his power over other people.'

'*Yah*,' said Simba, standing to his feet and reaching for his knobbed stick, 'behold, Bwana, he had been brought to the village by the relations of the Chief, and he will be one who opposes us in all that we shall attempt to do for God here.'

Then, in a voice that trembled somewhat: 'Bwana, a spell will be cast, a spell against Perisi here.'

There was a long awkward silence. The fire burned low; Simba stirred it with his stick and told me his plans for his new house.

'Bwana,' he said, 'this will be a better house than anyone has ever built in this part of the country. I have not made it like they do, of wicker work, poles and mud, but I have built it with sun-dried bricks. For a week I make these, and then for a week I let them dry. While one batch is drying, behold, I build with the other lot, and Bwana, these are my plans for the rest of the house.' He threw some light wood on the fire and began tracing on the ground with the thin end of his stick.

'It will be a long house, with only one door. That will open into the middle room here where the food will be prepared and cooked.' He pointed to a longer room with no roof as yet. 'Bwana, this will be where we sleep. Behold, it will be such a room as is very strange in our country. Behold, there will be windows in it. The windows will be covered with wire to keep out the mosquitoes.'

'*Heeh*,' said Daudi, 'tell Bwana about your scheme for the window in your kitchen.'

Simba laughed. 'Behold, there will be a hole in the wall here which will be a window. Behold, there will be wire in that window too for most of the day, except the time when Perisi will be putting the flour through the sieve.'

'*Heh*,' I said, 'and why should there not be wire in the window while she does that?'

'Bwana,' laughed Simba, 'because the sieve will be the window. I will make it square, just to fit the hole, and when she has finished using it as a sieve it will go back as a window to keep out the flies and mosquitoes.'

'*Heh*,' I said, 'and what is the purpose of the third room you're going to build?'

Simba laughed, and looked across at Perisi. She too smiled.

'Bwana,' she said, 'That will be the children's room, the place where I shall show the mothers how to look after their babies. Behold, there will be a water-pot in one corner; the water will be boiled and will be covered so that no dirt will get into it. Simba will weave me a cot out of vines from the jungle. Behold, I shall have there a broom with which I shall sweep the house to keep it clean. *Kumbe*, there will be light and air in that room through the window. *Yah*, Bwana, the window will be closed with wire so that no snakes or insects can get in. It will show the people a new way of living.'

'*Kah*,' said Daudi, 'that is a very good idea. And many people will come to look at it, but behold, why is it a children's room if there are no children in it?'

Perisi looked across at the fire and smiled. '*Hongo*,' she said, 'it is our hope that before the days of Christmas are long passed there will be a child in that cradle.'

Simba was smiling all over his face. '*Yah*, Bwana, behold, we have joy.'

Then as we sat around the fire it seemed by mutual consent, our heads were bowed, and we asked the Almighty Father to bring His blessing upon that new life that was to occupy that new room in the new home. Very quietly Simba said: '*Heya*,' which is 'Amen' in Chigogo, and then he got to his feet.

'Bwana,' he said, his face shining. 'I can see big things likely to happen in the place where we are going. This will open up the new way and I feel that many people will want to follow the ways of God. How can they do otherwise?'

'I can understand your feeling that way, Simba, because, behold, you have chosen to follow God's way, which He says is a narrow and difficult path. It was at no small cost that you understood these things.'

Simba nodded and glanced across at his wife. The look that passed between them spoke volumes, and I thought of the day when his life had been in jeopardy and as blood transfusion had made all the difference.*

I turned over the pages of the Chigogo New Testament and read a few verses which had been translated into the everyday speech of the people. I put my finger on the place. 'Behold, God is speaking to the people through the mouth of Jesus. He is telling them of His kingdom in heaven. This is what He says to those who will travel the paths of this world: "Make your way in by the narrow gate, for it is a broad gate and a wide road that leads to destruction, and those who go in that way are many indeed; but how small is the gate and how narrow the road that leads to life, and how few there are that find it."'

'*Yah*,' said Simba, 'does that mean that God doesn't want very many people to come into His Kingdom?'

'No, not that at all, but He has given men the right to choose for themselves. Many choose the broad path, so slightly down hill, rather than the way of God which leads up hill, which takes courage, and which needs obedience to His orders. That is why there are so few who follow it. Make no mistake, Simba, this new job of yours is not going to be easy. There are two roads that people can follow. Behold, travelling along the broad

*See *Jungle Doctor Meets a Lion*

road, with its ways of witchcraft and of lust and of drunkenness, and its ways of laziness, of pride: *kumbe!* There are many that follow that way.'

Again there was a long silence, and again it was interrupted by the braying of a donkey.

'*Yah,*' I laughed, 'was it not a donkey that put a man on the right track in the days of the prophet, when …'

But Daudi interrupted me.

'Bwana,' he said urgently, 'that donkey did not sing its song because of any joy in its heart; behold, something disturbed it. There is somebody or something near to it.'

We threw some cornstalks on to the fire and it flared up, but nothing was to be seen.

'*Yah*, Daudi, there's something wrong with you tonight, and perhaps *izuguni*, the mosquito, has bitten you, and malaria is close.'

'*Ng'o,*' said the African, 'there is something about, something strange.'

And as he spoke the moon came from behind the clouds. Silhouetted against a gap in the hills was a short figure with a commanding bearing. A flame leaped up in the fire, and by it  I saw an African standing not twenty yards away. There was a cold, compelling gleam in his eyes. The flame died away and the dark figure merged into the shadows again.

'*Yah,*' said Daudi, in little more than a whisper, 'Bwana, that was Dawa, the witchdoctor.'

4

Fatal Stroke

Sechelela put her head out of the hospital kitchen.

'*Hongo*, Bwana, you arrive in time to hear the news.'

'*Eeh!*' said Perisi, raising her eyebrows, 'twins?'

'*N'go*,' laughed Sechelela, 'worse than that; the cook is sick.'

Perisi smiled. 'Is that bad news? Did I not hear that many were sick of her?'

'*Kumbe*,' said the old African nurse, 'Unless we can get someone to take her place there will be no food for the hospital.'

'Whom do you suggest, Sech? Who can cook *wugali*, porridge, but not create trouble with her tongue?'

Sechelela wrinkled her forehead in thought, and then said:

'Bwana, there is Raheli, the widow of Chamulomo. She is newly come to Mvumi and is staying with her relations down by the river. She is a good woman and a good cook. Her tongue is short.'

'Good, see if you can get her.'

Raheli was a fine soul. She did her work most effectively, without any trouble; cooking the great clay pots full of porridge for the patients was a thankless task. It meaning pounding the grain and then sieving off the husks, grinding the prepared millet seed, and then cooking masses of the thick porridge which is the chosen diet of the people of this part of the Central Plains of East Africa. It was always a source of wonderment to me that in our C.M.S. Hospital we could feed, please and satisfy eighty people for a day at a cost of six shillings, since a kerosene tin full of flour costs a shilling.

One morning Raheli burnt her hand, and as I dressed it she told me that she had come from a village twenty miles away, the village from which Majimbi had originally come. She smiled her thanks, and I felt that she was going to be a very real help to us. Then, one morning, Perisi came and said:

'Bwana, Raheli refuses to come to hospital.'

'Why, Perisi?'

She shrugged her shoulders, and I knew when she took that attitude, that the best thing to do was to say nothing, and wait. Raheli did not come to Church. I missed her from the chattering collection of women who walked past the hospital, on their way to the well, with their gourds on their heads and their children on their backs. There was a mystery about it all, but nobody seemed willing to say a word. I knew that, sooner or later, given the right backing, I would get the whole story out of somebody, so I bided my time.

To say things were hectic would be to put it mildly. With a sigh I wrote up the book –

Mabwaji - Twins	12.15 a.m.	M. & F.	6 lbs. each.
Tabu	1.00 a.m.	F.	7 ¼ lbs.
Tatu, Sister of Tabu	2.30 .am.	F.	9 lbs.

Mbeleje - After her name I wrote three full lines of medical detail, which covered four hours of hard work, and at the bottom:

8.15 p.m.	M.	Premy. 3 lbs.

A voice came to the door. 'Bwana, breakfast.'

I glanced at my watch; it was 10 a.m. I was still wearing yesterday's shirt and my chin had a liberal crop of stubble. I saw the old Matron passing. All night long we had worked together.

'Sech,' I asked, 'do you feel as I do? Would you like a cup of tea to chase your tiredness?'

She looked at the tray, a smile lighting up her wrinkled old face. 'Yes, Bwana, five teaspoonfuls of sugar for me.'

She stirred her cup of weak syrup and summed up my feelings admirably when she said:

'I wouldn't mind this night duty, Bwana, if we only worked at night.'

I was looking out of the window, and I saw Raheli go past. She looked ill. It was a most unusual hour of the day for a woman to be going to draw water. I poured out another cup of tea for the old woman.

'Sech, there's no one to hear; tell me the story of Raheli. Why has this change come? No longer is she happy; she goes nowhere.'

Sechelela got slowly to her feet, and peered first out of the door, and then looked through the window. She moved her stool closer to the table, and in a confidential whisper said: 'Bwana, it is a very bad matter. You cannot understand it, not being an African.'

'Tell me,' I urged, 'that at least I may know.'

'Bwana,' she said, 'do not tell who told you.'

She was obviously upset. She drank thirstily from her third cup, and then told me her story.

'It was this way, Bwana. While Raheli was cooking for us here, some strangers came to visit in Mvumi village. They came from a village far away. They are the relations of that troublemaker, Majimbi. One of them saw Raheli, and said:

"Oh, so she is here."

"Yes," said the woman. "Why, is …"

"*Kah*," replied the first woman. "Don't you know? The Chief ordered her mother to be killed. She is a witch; she casts spells." She shrugged her shoulders.

'And so the woman started talking. They went to the well, and as they pounded and ground, one said to the other: "Truly, there have been many tragic happenings, and, lately, did not our cow dry up suddenly?" "Yoh," said a second, "and now I come to think of it, did not our calf die for no reason at all?" "*Heee!*" said a third, "and did not Raheli's sister-in-law lose her baby? It suddenly became ill. They took it to the witchdoctor; he made medicine, but the baby died."'

I sniffed. 'I suppose, Sech, they crammed the poor little creature with porridge, and then poured goat's fat and poisonous herbs down its throat.'

The old African woman nodded. 'Probably, Bwana, or perhaps they tied a cowskin charm round its neck, and hoped that would cure his gastro-enteritis.'

She took up the thread of her story. 'And then, at the well that evening, they remembered other things. A child had broken his arm, and one of the wells in the river had suddenly become salt. For days the whole story simmered, and then, as Raheli went to the well, she found the women looking askance at her and walking away. No one would walk before her or behind her. They feared she would cast a spell. They told stories of childless mothers, who blamed Raheli for their trouble. They would say: "*Yoh*, let us hide; here comes the witch." Raheli said to them: "Behold, I am no witch," but they spat at her. She appealed to them, and: "I am a Christian," but it made no difference. Bwana, the things that we have learned to fear for centuries are wrapped round our hearts. When she went for firewood into the jungle, she went alone. No one would work with her in her garden. Bwana, Perisi and I have gone at night to comfort her, but she is fretting. She will die, Bwana, her heart is heavy. This is the work of Majimbi; she knows Raheli's story and works with great cunning.'

I went myself next day to the house. '*Hodi*?' I called, but there was no reply. Again I called: '*Hodi*, may I come in?'

This time from the smoky interior of the house came an unintelligible sound. I walked in, and there was Raheli, wrapped up in a dirty black cloth, lying on the floor. She was an utter contrast to the woman who had recently helped us so ably at the hospital. She had aged ten years in as many days. I spoke to her, but she just shook her head. I talked to her of God, and of His power, but again she shook her head. At last with a feeling of absolute inability to do anything I got up to go.

I sometimes wonder whether I should have done what I did next. I saw a hospital nurse, dressed in black, coming furtively to the house. She did not see me, but slipped in, as she thought, unnoticed. She squatted down beside the woman, who lay motionless on the floor. Tender terms of endearment came from her lips. 'I do not fear you, little mother,' she said; 'do not grieve at the vain words of the women.'

Raheli shook her head, and in a flat, toneless voice said:

'I am alone in the world; alone at the firewood, alone in the garden, alone in the home. My heart is alone, my husband's relations are frightened of me. My children have been sent to relatives. I am weary of life; I long for death.'

'But,' said Perisi, 'do you not fear the hereafter?'

The woman shook her head. 'Why should I?'

'But listen,' said Perisi again in a firm voice. 'I could shake you! Let the Bwana take you to a new country, to the C.M.S. Hospital at Kilimatinde. It is a hundred miles away.'

Raheli shook her head. 'Are not tongues longer than that? Do not words fly like dust storms?'

'*Hongo*,' replied the nurse, 'His Book says: "Let not your heart be troubled."'

Raheli stood up. '*Mwanagu*, my child, I long to be with God. I cannot bear to live as I am living, and you must not come, for they will say that you, too, are a witch – you whose life has been painful from birth – you, too, have yet to suffer untold things.'

Perisi stepped back involuntarily.

'I have no fear for the future. My life is in the hands of my Father, God.'

Raheli went on unheeding in her weak, sing-song voice.

'My days are few; your days are many.'

The effort seemed to have cost her much. She sat down again. 'Bring me water.' Perisi held a gourd to her mouth. She drank thirstily. There was the noise of someone walking past in the darkness and then came a cackle of horrible laughter. My skin crept. I heard a gasp from Perisi. She pulled her black hood over her head and ran through the door into the gloom.

That evening, at home, I sat listening to a performance of a Beethoven Symphony, from New York, on short wave, and as I turned it off, I heard weird singing, the throb of dancing feet and, above it all, a ghastly wailing sound. The drums stopped, and the night was still in a sinister way. I wondered what it all meant.

Next morning, I heard that Raheli was dead, and once again I plied Sechelela with tea and questions. But this time she, too, was silent. She shook her head.

'Bwana, you are a European. You can speak our language, and understand us a little, but how can you know Chigogo *chetu*, our customs, our life? There are things too dark for a white man's mind to grasp.'

I watched her walk slowly back to superintend the bathing of the African babies, and I thought of the tragedies hidden in those mud huts that basked in the bright sunlight of Equatorial Africa.

In the burning heat of midday I saw Majimbi walk boldly up to the hospital, pause, and then spit on the wall. Again came the same harsh cackle of laughter that I had heard the night before. Daudi put down his test tube and said: '*Yoh*, Bwana, truly that woman of trouble feels she had double revenge. We must be very, very careful.'

5

Rubbish to Rejoicing

'*Yah*,' said Perisi, '*yah*, that Majimbi is a bad one.'

'*Hum, nhawule*, what's up now?' I asked, without looking up from the microscope through which I was examining a sample of a baby's blood and hunting for malaria bugs.

Perisi's voice was indignant. 'Bwana, *Wataga mwana ayu, makatye yono yali manyagala nyagala, ninga yali mwana swanu.* They threw out this child, they said he was just "no person," and rubbish, but he's beautiful.'

She made noises that women, the world over, make when they have a baby in their arms.

'*Hongo*,' said Sechelela, with such vigour that her latest grandchild asleep on her back, kept there by the African variety of cuddle seat, opened one sleepy eye in wonderment at the strange sounds which her grandmother was producing.

'*Yoh!* Rubbish, indeed; look at the baby, Bwana.'

I did. It wasn't very big, perhaps a four-pounder, and the poor little girl had a harelip.

'Rubbish!' said Perisi with fine scorn, rocking the baby to and fro and proceeding to give a further assortment of maternal noises.

'*Hongo!* And what are you going to do about it?'

Perisi tossed her head. '*Heeh*, Bwana you…' and then seeing the smile around my lips she smiled too.

'*Kumbe*, I thought you were going to say it was a child of no value.'

The baby gave a rather peculiar cry.

'You see, this child can't drink properly. I tried her on a bottle and she couldn't swallow and nearly choked. I held her by the feet and let it trickle out and so, Bwana, I brought her to you. If it's just a matter of feeding babies' – she smiled all over her cheerful African face – 'I know how to do that.'

'Bring the baby over here into the light,' I said.

Quite frankly, I did not feel too happy about it. What I feared was a palate split right down and I had visions of feeding the child through a tube for months and months, and I knew we had only one such tube in the hospital.

Gently Perisi's finger pushed the baby's mouth open. The lip was undoubtedly unsightly, but the palate was whole, except for a dimple at the back which was of little importance.

'*Hongo*,' I said, 'there's one thing I want you always to remember when you examine a baby. If it's a boy it doesn't matter much, but if it's a girl you must always do it, it's vitally important. And if you don't do it, well…' I shrugged my shoulders, and Perisi's face was very serious.

'Bwana,' she said, 'I wish you had more opportunity of teaching us things, but you are so busy operating and mixing medicines and looking down microscopes and running round Tanganyika in the car that rattles to the other hospitals, that you seldom can teach us the finer points.'

'This is a fine point, Perisi. You must always look very carefully at the tongue of any female child.'

'*Yah*,' said Sechelela, 'men talk just as much as women.'

I put back my head and laughed. '*Huh*, you always bite, Sech – you always bite. Look at this little person, see? Her tongue just won't move, but I'll deal with it.'

An hour later in the Baby Welfare Room I addressed a group of ten nurses, their faces contrasting with their white uniforms and caps.

'I want each of you to look at this baby's tongue. I want you with your right hand to feel your own tongue, feel underneath it. Can you feel how it's tied down with that thin curtain of flesh?'

There was an opening of mouths and a waggling of fingers, and a nodding of heads.

'Now,' I said, 'feel the baby's tongue, but not with the same hand!'

This was duly done. A few drops of anaesthetic were sufficient to make sure that the poor little scrap of humanity should suffer no pain, and one of the most minor surgical operations was performed. The African nurses crowded round.

'There,' I said, 'the tongue moves.'

A quarter-of-an-hour later Perisi, sitting on a wooden stool, was feeding the baby from a bottle. A beaming smile on the African girl's face indicated that my surgical handiwork had been successful.

'*Yah*,' said she, 'we are out of the thorns now; the baby will grow. I'll look after this child myself. Behold, in the village three miles away they have sadness in their hearts because the child is no more, but we will feed her and build her up and then what joy to the mother, and *yah*, what confusion to those old women, Majimbi and her cronies, when we bring a child back from the dead, as it were.'

'But how did you get hold of the baby, Perisi? You didn't steal it or snatch it, did you?'

The nurse shook her head vigorously. '*N'go*, Bwana, they put the baby out in the cold in the dark, and they think that a hyena has taken it.'

'But who did take it?'

Perisi smiled. 'It's all the fault of the C.M.S. School. They bring children from the villages, they teach them baby welfare, they bring them to the hospital. See what they do?'

I looked through the window and there were six girls from the Mvumi C.M.S. Girls' Boarding School, all bathing babies in the approved fashion.

'You see,' went on Perisi, 'there was young Merabi, the younger sister of the mother of this child. She heard the words of the old women; she heard the weeping of her sister; so she crept round, wrapped the child in a blanket, and ran through the darkness to my house.'

'But what about the child's mother?'

Perisi shook her head. '*Yoh*, Bwana, a sad case. She's the third wife of an old man, who beats her. This is her fourth child and all the others have died. She believes she's bewitched and she just lies in bed, listless. Does she not walk with a limp and is she not the scorn of the other women in her house?'

That baby grew. It was fed religiously at six, ten, two, six and ten. It was test-weighed, put down to sleep, not unduly fussed over, everything was done that should have been done, in just the way that it should have been done. Perisi saw to that! And then one day I operated again, this time to repair the ugly gash of the hare-lip. The result was considerably better than I had hoped. Ten days later I removed the stitches and Perisi looked at her charge.

'There,' she said, 'is she not beautiful?'

I grinned. 'Go on. Make all the clucking noises that your tongue makes, like a hen!'

'*Yah*,' said Perisi indignantly, 'you are only a man!'

Then she smiled. 'Bwana, today is going to be a great day. I feel my skin is too tight for the joy that I have within it.'

I laughed. 'What's up?'

'Bwana, Mavunde, the baby's mother, is coming to the hospital today. She's losing weight; she's sick, she's wretched, she's without hope, she longs to die even as Raheli.'

'*Hongo*,' I said, 'so you are bringing her to the hospital. Do you think we can help her to die here?'

'*Yoh*,' said Perisi, 'will you be serious, Bwana? The cause of her sadness is the loss of her baby. She doesn't want medicine; she wants the gap in her life filled; and how we will fill it!'

I kept Mavunde waiting until I had dealt with all the usual malarias and fevers, coughs, colds, tropical eye-disease and the whole usual collection of out-patients' work. She limped into the room and sat down.

'*Utamigweci*, what's your complaint?' I asked.

She shook her head. 'Bwana, I cannot sleep. I have no desire for food, I want to die.'

'*Hongo*,' I said, 'why?'

She shook her head. 'You are only a man, you wouldn't understand.'

'Mavunde,' I said, 'it might be that after you told me I could help.'

For a while she hesitated, and then came the whole grim story of the young wife of an old husband, the domination of the old women, and their ghastly habits and tricks, the story of dead baby after dead baby.

'Bwana, it's six weeks ago now since my baby was born. They took it from me; they said it was dead. I don't know if it was a boy or a girl. I only knew that its face was scarred and that it was very small. Bwana, when I was at school I heard them pray. I laughed then; but these days I have prayed, and God has not answered.'

'It is not enough to pray. First you must join God's tribe, you must give your life to Him, and then you have a right to pray.'

'I would, Bwana, if my baby was alive.'

'Go and eat with the hospital people, your old friends from school, and I'll see you again this afternoon.'

It was an hour later than I heard a peculiar shrill sound made by African women who are happy.

Into my office came Perisi and Mavunde, a very different Mavunde. No word was said, but there was a look in her eyes that was worth all that we had done.

That evening Perisi said: 'Bwana, it has been a happy month. Behold, my heart has much joy in it tonight.'

And although I was a mere man, mine felt just the same way.

As I walked to the gate Daudi ran out. 'Bwana, I hear words of warning. Majimbi has great anger because of the work of the hospital.'

I raised my eyebrows. 'This harelipped baby, eh?'

Daudi nodded. 'That, Bwana, and the child with pneumonia, and the baby we operated on, and ...' he

paused. '*Kah*, Bwana, so many things happen for the benefit of children here. Do we not overshadow the work of Majimbi and her helpers? And for this reason they have anger.'

6

Pulling the Curtain Aside

A week went by. I fumbled with the door of the operating theatre and blinked as I came out into the bright sunlight. My head was covered with an operating cap and my nose and mouth were behind a gauze mask. An African greeted me.

'*Mbukwa*, Bwana.'

'*Mbukwa*,' I replied, 'Good day.'

He looked at me. '*Kah*, Bwana, why do you hide your face in this fashion?'

'Behold,' I said, 'when we bring medicine to people and we have to adjust things within them, we cover our mouths from germs, little things, smaller than anything. Our eyes cannot see them, but they are there, and they're more dangerous than hyenas and leopards, and snakes and spiders.'

As I said this I recognized him. 'Do you not remember this, was it not your child who needed our help the other day? Did he not suffer from very bad complaints inside, and was he not very sick?'

I took off the mask and cap.

'*Yah*,' said the man. 'Behold, Bwana, we have great joy in our house. Did I not go back to my village? Have I not brought you a gift for the hospital?'

I noticed a young bull tied by the back legs in the corner of the hospital courtyard.

'Bwana, we have great joy in the village, and my family have sent *ngombe*, a cow, that you may have profit in your work.'

'*Hongo*,' I said, 'we do not seek profit for our work, but we do appreciate your kindness.'

From round the corner of the hospital came his wife with her baby, now a very prosperous-looking citizen, on her back, smiling contentedly over her shoulder, and making the noises that babies make when they're happy.

I called the staff together. 'Behold, we have joy in our hearts. Is not a child restored to health? Is not his father filled with happiness and his mother – has she joy?'

'*Yah*,' said the women, 'Bwana, has she joy? Behold her heart sings within her.'

It seemed that the singing was infectious because the bull, tied outside, suddenly commenced to bellow.

'Bwana,' said the father, 'behold, many of us had a hand in helping the child. Daudi here prepared carefully the medicine. It was Yohanna that drew water from the well that we made the medicines from.'

Yohanna, the water-carrier, had only one eye but he had a very real idea of his function in life. 'Yes,' he

said, 'Bwana, I make fifteen journeys a day. Is it not my way of saying "thank you" to God that I have one eye left that works?'

I stopped him just in time, because once you encouraged Yohanna, he would go on for ever.

'But it was Perisi who took the biggest share of all in nursing him.'

'Bwana,' said Sechelela, 'do not forget that if we had not asked the help of God, and if we had not lived in God's way, the child would never have recovered. Is it the custom of our tribe for another woman to look after a child who is no relation of hers?'

The woman shook her head. 'Truly, this is so.'

'*Hongo*,' went on Sechelela, 'but it is God's way.' She turned to the mother. 'Do you understand these things now?'

The mother nodded. '*Heya*, yes, have I not spoken with you many times during the hours of the night? Will I not go to speak to Perisi when she comes to the village where I live – Makali?'

'Shall I listen to the words of the women?' asked the husband, taking a deliberate pinch of snuff.

Daudi answered swiftly. 'Does not Simba the lion-hunter live in your village? Is he not building his *kaya* there these days? Is not Perisi returning tomorrow to live there?'

'*Hongo*,' said the African, picking up his spear and knobbed stick. '*Ale chaherera*, we will set on our way.'

Daudi came over and whispered in my ear: 'Bwana, what are you going to do with the bull?'

'Will we not keep it here and look at it every day? Behold, will it not be very good food for the eyes?'

Daudi looked at me and smiled. 'Bwana, do I not understand the thoughts of your heart? Is it that this cow will find its way into a pot and will come out with very thick gravy?'

I nodded. 'See if this man will not stay with his wife and enjoy the feast we will have. Will we not have great joy?'

A high-pitched voice behind me called: 'Bwana, *mwana yunji manghye*. Doctor, another baby; run.'

I jumped to my feet and saw the grinning face of Simba.

'*Kah*, you! You're no baby; you must have smelled this feast.'

The African laughed. 'Bwana, my house is finished enough for Perisi to live in it. I have come for her.'

'*Swanu*,' I replied, 'Good. This shall be a farewell party.'

There was tremendous activity in the kitchen. I got two kerosene tins full of millet grain especially for the feast. These cost the large sum of two shillings each. The staff and convalescent patients got to work and prepared all this, and it was ground to fine flour.

They cooked great pots full of *wugali*, native porridge, and other great pots containing various titbits let forth delicious odours. Small boys hovered round the place and wrinkled their noses in keen appreciation. At sundown the whole feast was ready. Before we started, I turned to everybody.

'Behold, has not our friend here shown his thankfulness that his child is better in a very practical way? What could be more attractive to the nose than this *muhuzi*, this gravy?'

There were appreciative and agreeable sounds.

I continued. 'Before we have our feast let us, too, say "thank you" to God for His goodness to us.'

'Bwana, before you do that,' said the woman who had looked so dull a little while before, 'Bwana, I would tell everybody before my husband here, that the words of God have sunk deep into my heart. I have heard of His love and now my heart sings with thanks to Him. Behold, I will live His way.'

A silence fell on the gathering, and in that silence I prayed very quietly that God would bless us all, and give us very thankful hearts; and then we got to

work on the feast. It was amazing to see it disappear. A petrol lantern was brought out and hung up, and then the folk started singing.

'Bwana,' called a voice, '*Use mbera*, you are wanted here quickly.'

'*Yah*,' said Sechelela, 'more babies.'

Two hours later the old African matron, Perisi, and Mwendwa, who was to take her place, stood with me looking out over the now-quiet hospital courtyard. Three great empty clay pots were all that remained of the feast.

7

Attack with Poison

'*Koh*, Bwana,' said old Sechelela. She stirred the sugar vigorously in her handleless cup. '*Koh*, there is great trouble looming over our heads. We would not have known a word about it but for that child.' She pointed with her chin towards a cot where a newborn baby was voicing strong protest to the world at large.

'*Hongo*, Sech,' I said, 'you talk in riddles. Tell me what it all means.'

'*Koh*,' said the old African matron, 'for four long and bitter days, Bwana, the old women of that child's mother's village did everything that they knew, but still the child did not arrive.'

I nodded. Behind the old African woman's words there was as grim a picture of hopeless suffering and hopeless ignorance as it is possible to find.

The old African nurse went on. 'Bwana, for two days the child's mother was given nothing to drink, but behold, in the dark of the night quietly one came to her and gave her water from a gourd and told her that only here, in our C.M.S. hospital, was there safety and hope. Even then, Bwana, it seemed to her that the voice of her ancestors was calling her. That was not to be, for Perisi heard these words, and visited her secretly. Perisi gave her words of comfort, and told her of the God who cared. Then it would seem that, as they spoke, one of the old women stirred in her sleep and woke. Perisi slipped out of the house, but the old women became suspicious. Ndebeto, the child's mother, heard the old women speak many words that night and the next day.

'"*Yoh*," said one old woman, "she comes to our village, a young married woman, to teach us, the wise ones, the ways of children. She would steal from us the trust of the younger women."

'"*Heh*," broke in another, "behold, the way of our wealth will disappear."

'Then one of them said: "*Heh*, shall she herself have living children? Shall she show us a living child of her own, and the words she speaks of feeding a child with milk and not with porridge? Behold, a spell has been cast, and she shall carry no child upon her back."'

Sechelela shook her head. 'Bwana, these are the words that Ndebeto heard.'

'*Yoh*,' I said, 'but why then did Ndebeto come here?'

'Behold, Bwana, she spoke many words in the ear of her husband. Was her husband not saved from the disease you call pneumonia through our pills at the hospital, and did he not agree to bring her in? Did they not travel through the night and arrive here three hours before the dawn?'

'*Eh-heh*,' I said, ' and did I not get up when the night was old and come to the hospital and kill a snake on the path?'

'*Eh, eeeh*,' said Sechelela, 'a snake on the path is a small thing when you remember that at the dawning, through your work, that child was born safely and alive just in time to see the sunrise. This was a work that none but a doctor could do.'

'Truly,' I replied, 'but if you hadn't been there, and the others, and we hadn't had the medicine, where would we have been and where would Ndebeto have been?'

Sechelela shook her head quietly. 'Bwana, she would truly have been with her ancestors now. There would be weeping throughout her family. The old women would sit around their fire and say that a spell had been cast against her.'

'And now, Ndebeto is well, and the baby sounds all right; listen to him.'

Sechelela smiled.

'But do you think, Sech, that Perisi will be in danger? You don't think that they will do any harm to her in that village, or to Simba?'

'Perhaps, Bwana, they will put poison in their food, but I doubt it. Behold, there will be many spells cast. Her life will be a very hard one these days.'

'There is one thing we can do to protect them, Sech.'

She raised her eyebrows questioningly.

'Once there was one of God's teachers named Elisha who lived in the days of a very bad chief. This chief was very angry, because every time he planned a wrongdoing, the teacher knew of it. God told him. So

71

he planned to kill the teacher. He sent his soldiers, very many of them all very strongly armed, and they came at night and surrounded the city on the hill where he was. Behold, in the morning the teacher's servant, a young man, woke very early, and as the sun rose he saw the shields and spears of the soldiers round about the village. He was terrified. He said: "What will we do? Oh, my master!" But Elisha said to God: "O Great One, open his eyes." And it was as though a mist seemed to clear away from the young man's eyes and he saw, behind the soldiers of the bad chief, that the whole mountain was full of men on horses, very strong soldiers, a host of heaven sent there by God to protect Elisha, who was God's servant. Then again the great prophet said: "Behold, we have nothing to fear. Those that are with us are more than those that are with them."'

The old woman nodded. '*Heh – heh*, Bwana, and Elisha escaped.'

'Scissors, Sech, where are my Number One best pair?'

'*Yoh*,' said the old African nurse, 'I saw Elizabeth with the one eye about to cut her hair with them so I hid them in my room in the basket under my bed amongst some shelled peanuts.'

'Will you get them for me, Sech?'

'Behold, Bwana, I have only just started to bathe these babies and the nurses are having a special afternoon pass to play basketball at the School.'

I went out of the surgery thinking of my best surgical scissors when Daudi came up. 'Bwana, I saw Majimbi come out of the nurses' dormitory.'

'*Kah*, Daudi, she is full of all manner of doings. Let us look round.'

I half expected to find a fire or a snake but there was no sign of any mischief. As I looked under a nurse's bed and found a pile of peanut shells I suddenly remembered my scissors and turned to Daudi.

'Elizabeth was going to cut her hair with our best scissors!'

'*Yoh*,' laughed the dispenser, 'she is looking for trouble.'

I nodded. 'And she found it when Sech saw her.' I raised my eyebrows . . .

'And where did the hospital's grandmother hide them, Bwana?'

I laughed. 'In a basket of peanuts; come and help me get them.'

There was no door into Sechelela's cubicle, but a brand new and very stylish printed cotton curtain. As I entered the room the hem of the material brushed against my hand. Cautiously I felt it, and then, with a grunt of surprise, slit down the hem with a penknife. Three rusty razor blades tinkled to the floor. They were smeared with black grease.

'My word, Daudi, that's dangerous. Anyone could have cut themselves badly.'

Very carefully I picked up the rusty blades and slipped them into a matchbox. This was hardly in my pocket when Sechelela called, '*Hodi*? May I come in?' – at the door.

'*Karibu*,' I replied, 'Come in.' She pushed aside the curtain, and I could not help noticing how her hand closed tightly over the hem of the curtain, which a few minutes before had held hidden those sharp slithers of steel, which now reposed in my pocket.

'Sech, do you always grasp the curtain like that when you come in?'

She smiled up at me, and her face was a very comely one.

'I've never noticed, Bwana. Yes, when I come to think of it, that is my habit.'

Daudi raised his eyebrows!

Late that afternoon, with test tubes, flasks, and sundry bottles of chemicals around me, I tested the edge of one of the razor blades. I watched the contents of the flask bubbling gaily over a little spirit lamp.

'Oh, Daudi, where did you put the other blades?'

'They're safe, Bwana. I left them in the

matchbox on the very top of a cupboard in my house.'

'Your children couldn't get at them?'

'Oh no, Bwana, it is high up. I had to stand on a chair which I had placed on a petrol box to reach the top.'

I decanted a little of the fluid, and whistled quietly. 'You're right, Daudi; it is a poison. Probably a drug we call *strophanthus*. It causes the heart to go into a sort of cramp, and that is the end.'

'I thought as much, Bwana, but how can you prove it?'

'Sechelela went very close to proving it today.'

About a fortnight later a patient came in from a strange tribe and with him he brought a diminutive monkey, which was the worry of our life, but the joy of the small boy whose life had been in the balance. Samson was terrified that the little creature would get in amongst his bottles in the dispensary. Already he had done no little damage to the cooking-pots in the nurses' kitchen, and so we were quite prepared for a commotion outside. But we were not prepared for what we saw. The little creature was lying on the ground, surrounded by the usual collection of patients and small boys. Its limbs were moving convulsively, and the palm of its hand was gashed where it had cut itself with one of the razor blades that Daudi had so carefully stored away.

A small boy moved across to pick up the blade. I leapt across.

'Don't touch it, there's death in it.'

The crowd backed away hurriedly. The little creature shuddered and lay dead. With a pair of forceps I picked up the blades and carried them away. Daudi called Sechelela and pointed to the dead animal. I showed her the test I had made.

'Sechelela, there are people who are trying to kill you with poison.'

She nodded simply. 'Yes, Bwana, I thought that might happen, but, Bwana, do we not remember that Elisha escaped? Was not his life in God's hands, and is not mine?'

8

Progress and Setback

Things were quiet in the hospital. At *nzogolo*, first cock-crow, we had set out on a safari to Makali, and had pulled up on the side of a hill overlooking the village. It was a magnificent view. Daudi and I stood in the early morning looking due east over line after line of hills that sloped brown at first, and then pale blue into the distance. Far away against the horizon, a hundred miles away, I could see the faint outline of the Uluguru Mountains from the peaks of which I knew you could see the Indian Ocean.

Daudi and I walked up to the summit of a granite-crowned peak that stood out above the plains of Central Tanganyika. With no little difficulty we scrambled up the side of the huge granite boulders to get this wonderful view.

'*Yah*,' said the dispenser, 'this is the place to start a village hospital, the place to start a work for God. Behold a small hospital, Bwana, and a school, and between them a church that people may have their bodies mended and their minds enlightened, so that in doing these two things, Bwana, light may come to their soul.'

As I stood there I thought of the days when H.M. Stanley had travelled through that very same valley, and had been met with nothing but hostility from the ancestors of the very people we were now working with. When he had travelled there had been danger from spears and demands for money to let him pass with safety. But now there were leaders among the tribes like Daudi and Simba, men who were anxious to take the lead in helping their own people. From my pocket I took a folded piece of ancient paper that had come from a white-ant-eaten copy of Stanley's book *Through Darkest Africa*. I read a sentence or two.

'Listen, Daudi, this is what the great pioneer, Bwana Stanley, said about this country at which we are looking. He wrote: "This is a country of vile water, myriad insects, irritating to the point of madness, a ferment of trouble and distraction, and a vermin of petty annoyances to any traveller entering the country. No natives know better how to be unpleasant to travellers. One would think there is a school somewhere in Ugogo to teach low cunning and vicious malice to the people."'

Daudi threw back his head and laughed. '*Hah*, Bwana,' he said, 'Stanley knew little of our people. *Heh*, but he certainly didn't know where the right wells were. Behold, he didn't have the people to help him as you have these days.'

We looked at the villages dotted here and there over the vast area. Then Daudi took me round to the other side of the hill.

'Bwana, here is a thing you have not seen before.'

As I looked my heart sank. In a hollow on the hill was an old building, obviously built by a European. It had a rusty, dilapidated tin roof and there were great gaping holes in the wall. Beyond it were groves of mango trees and a circular stone wall that looked like a well. Still farther on was a native-built mud-walled grass-thatched building, roof half fallen in, with a cross lying at a crazy angle surmounting it.

'*Hongo*, what's this place, Daudi?'

'Come and see, Bwana.'

We went down the hill. My heart was very heavy as I looked at the ruins, a decaying monument to one of the tragedies of missionary service. The wiles of the witchdoctor and the shortage of European staff had led to the abandoning of this forward position. We came first to the wrecked church. I looked up mutely to see the white-ant-eaten cross, the rotting iron of the roof. I ducked my head down and walked into the building to be met full in the face with the ugly body of a great bat, one of the scores that flapped round in the semi-darkness of the place. Hurriedly I went outside.

'*Yah*, this is not a good place.'

'Bwana, this is the place where Simba plans to work. Behold, there is a well here.'

We went across to the place where the mango trees were, and looked down the well. A musty unwholesome smell came to us. We went across to the old house. It was a wreck. The floors for the most part had been destroyed by white ants, the ceiling sagged, and daylight could be seen in various places. I went out of the place with as heavy a heart as I had ever experienced in Africa, to be met at the door by the smiling face of Simba.

'Bwana,' he said, 'here's the place to start a church. Here's the place to build a school. *Yah*, there's a well over there. Much of the stone from this house we can use to build our foundations. Behold, we can repair the church. The walls are good. With some more iron for the roof we'll have all we want.'

'But the church is a wreck, Simba. There are white ants everywhere, and there are bats in the place. Behold, the well is full of mud and the place smells evil. There is no joy or comfort in that old home. Behold, it looks like the skeleton of one who should be living, smiling.'

Simba shook his head. 'Bwana, you must not look at it that way. Things are different. The well is full of mud and slush, but I will dig it out and use that mud and slime to make bricks.'

'*Kumbe*,' I said, still feeling keenly despondent, 'the water will not be good even then.'

'Bwana,' said Perisi, who had on her head a gourd full of water she had just brought from the well, 'the water will be good enough to mix with further mud to make more bricks, and by the time Simba has used enough water and mud to make many bricks, behold, the water will be sweet then and clear.'

'*Hongo*, Perisi,' I said, 'you've got the right end of the stick. Behold, did not King Daudi write very true words when he said: "Happy is the man whose strength is in God, and in whose heart are the highways to Zion. Who, passing through the valley of weeping, uses it for a well." *Heh*, don't you see it? Instead of just going through being mournful, he says: "This is a dark place, perhaps, and full of evil things, but behold, there is water here, I will stoop and fill my water bottle," and so when he comes to the dry plains he has water.'

'*Heeh*,' said Simba, 'that is what I seek to do. There will be much trouble from the witchdoctor, from the headman of the tribe. But, Bwana, we will work amongst the children and younger people and behold, there will rise up those who know God. This is our work.'

We walked down towards the village. In front of us was a typical African house with its mud walls and mud roof, built in a square with the cattle-yard in the centre. Looking through the opening that led into the place where the animals sat we saw a cowskin pegged out, a cowskin that had been torn.

'*Yah*,' said I, 'they don't take much care of their cowhides here.'

'*Kumbe*,' said Simba, 'there is a story to that, Bwana. It was but two days ago, when, at this time of the day, the woman who lives in that house came through the door and found four lions tearing at that cowhide. *Yah*, Bwana, she rushed into the house and she screamed at the top of her voice, but the lions took no notice, they tore the skin, and then the men came with spears, and the lions went back to the jungle. Behold, this is a place of animals.'

From somewhere inside that house came a pitiful cry of a child in pain. Simba went to the door and said:

'*Hodi*? May I come in?'

A minute later a small boy was brought out, his face grimy and tear-stained, his hand over his left ear.

'*Wusungu wuwaha*, great pain.' Speaking to his mother I said: 'Let him come with us to the car. Behold, there I have medicine, it may help him.'

I expected a long *shauri*, a discussion; but she said: 'Bwana, I agree. Behold, did I not get medicine that helped me greatly when I had a cough?'

The child walked along with his hand in Perisi's, telling me how the pain kept him awake night after night. Gently I looked into his ear. He had an abscess. Now the open air, in the heat of the Central African sun, surrounded by a considerable number of flies, is not what I regard as an ideal operating theatre. But by the side of car, with the little chap lying on a blanket, I did a minor operation. A whiff or two of chloroform and the small boy was asleep. The job was soon over, and a large white bandage was put around his head. A moment or two later when he came back to consciousness, he put his hand up gingerly to his ear.

'*Yah*, Bwana, it no longer throbs.' A smile came over his face. This must have been the first smile for days.

I gave him some pills to swallow and instructions that he was to come again that evening.

'*Eh*, Bwana,' he said. 'I'll do that.' A little lump of sugar was helpful.

Simba got to work that morning scooping mud out of the well and making bricks. About a hundred-and-fifty of them lay drying in the sun by evening. Simba with a grunt of satisfaction stretched his back and said:

'Bwana, that's work. But behold, I will now be able to start my building in a few days.'

That night I couldn't sleep. At midnight I got out of bed and went outside. The moon was bright. I looked over towards Simba's brickworks by the well. As I looked a shadow seemed to move out from the other shadows by the mango trees and I saw a small, solidly-built man deliberately walk right along the bricks that Simba had made, crushing them with his feet. Even at that distance I could recognize Dawa, the witchdoctor.

9

Risky Footwork

A large grey lizard stood on a flat stone, its throat pulsating. In the sunlight of the early African morning its shadow looked enormous against the dilapidated mudbrick wall of the house. I looked up towards the well, and could see what should have been the orderly rows of bricks made the day before – it was nothing but a mass of trampled mud now. In the thornbush on the hill above me a small bird gave its characteristic warble *'ndudududu.'*

And as if in answer from behind me came another *'ndudududu.'*

Before I could start any conjectures in the realm of bird lore I heard a deep voice behind me.

'Mbukwa, Bwana, does not the voice of the *ndudumizi* bird tell us that the rains are near?'

I turned round to see the smiling face of Simba. He pursed his lips and made the bird-call once again …'*ndudududu*.' '*Yah*, Bwana, what a morning. Behold, a day of rejoicing.'

I pointed down to where he had spent the whole of the day before hard at work. 'Perhaps your rejoicing will not last long when you see that.'

'*Kah*,' said Simba, 'for the second day my work has been ruined. *Yah*, this is the work of one who wishes us ill.'

Immediately above him came again the song of the *ndudumizi* bird. I turned round to see the little creature preening its feathers as it perched on one of the spikes of a great cactus. As I looked, suddenly an idea was borne in my mind, and I laughed.

'*Kumbe*, Simba, is it not true that wet bricks are soft to the feet?'

'*Heeh*,' said the African hunter, 'this is true, Bwana. If this is the work of Dawa he has nothing to fear, as far as the bruising of his feet are concerned, on my bricks. There are no stones in them, all the earth is carefully sifted . . .'

And then he followed my eyes to the cactus. He looked at it for a moment and suddenly burst into laughter. '*Heeh* …!' he said. This was too much for the lizard. It scrambled hastily for safety under a sisal bush. Simba clapped his hands together, rolled his eyes, and roared with laughter again. '*Heeh*, I see it. You suggest that we make a batch of bricks and put thorn in some of them, thorn covered carefully by the mud.'

I nodded. 'This should make him smile.'

'But behold, Bwana, will it be with laughter that he roars when he walks tonight on my bricks? Will he see the point of this joke?'

He slapped himself heartily on the chest.

'*Heeh*,' he said, 'this is a way of guile.'

Round the corner of the building came the face of an African boy. Simba saw him at once. '*Kah*, Bwana, I forgot. Behold, have I not brought a child to you today who is in much trouble? Behold, his skin is of the sort that must be scratched very frequently.'

The boy was entirely dressed in a miserable little black rag that made me itchy to look at it. His body was covered with sores and his fingers seemed automatically to seek out another spot to scratch. Carefully I examined him and turned to Daudi who had come out with a box of medicines and bandages.

'Scabies, plus infection. A nasty mess, but he'll clear up in a day or two, especially if that new medicine is any good. Bath him, Daudi, and then I'll paint him.'

The bath consisted of half-a-kerosene tin of lukewarm water, an empty condensed milk tin and a cake of carbolic soap. I pulled the cork from a bottle of milk-like fluid, and cutting a collection of twigs, the length of a pencil and the thickness of a match, I turned them into swab sticks by putting some cotton wool round the end and twisting it tightly. There was a pile of these beside me in a few moments. The African lad was lying in the warm sunlight. I put some of my swabs into the mixture and came over to him. I was going to paint it all over the spots where he had irritation.

'*Yeh*, Bwana, there will be pain.'

'*Uh, uh*,' I said, shaking my head, 'There will be none of that.'

'*Yah*, Bwana, but I am frightened.'

'There is no need to be frightened, there will be no pain whatever.'

The lad composed himself and set his teeth. I painted one arm with the mixture. '*Yah*,' he said, 'behold, it hurts no more than if it were milk.'

'Right! May I continue with the painting?'

'*Heeh*, Bwana.'

Before long, he had been covered from top to toe with this mixture which was death for that industrious little creature which burrows under the skin, and itches and itches and itches.

I had just finished when Daudi appeared with the condensed milk tin. From its steaming interior he withdrew the dirty black rag that the boy had worn round his middle.

'Bwana,' he said, 'it is the instruction that all clothing shall be boiled when people have scabies. I have boiled his clothing.'

There was a smile on the African dispenser's face. The rag was put out to dry. The boy went to pick it up.

'Wait a minute,' I said, 'you have only had half your painting.'

'*Yah*,' he said, 'this medicine will sting.'

I took a bright violet concoction from the second bottle and smeared it all over him. He looked the most peculiar colour, but once again he was fully confident when he found that this medicine didn't hurt either.

'*Kah*, Bwana,' he said, 'I trust you. I see that your way is a good one.'

'*Heh*,' said Simba, 'behold, if the Bwana says it, it's true.'

Simba had already gone down to the well and was busy making a huge pile of mud before moulding more bricks to replace those that had been ruined the night before. In the middle of this procedure he suddenly burst into a roar of laughter – '*Heeeeh!*'

He went to a spot where he could be seen only from where we stood and cut a series of very interesting looking thorns at least two inches long with his hunter's knife. He collected bunches of them so made that whichever way you stood them they would be sure to stick into you. They looked like gigantic pieces of barbed wire. After that he put some of the mud into the moulds and carefully pushed into them a big bunch of thorns. He smoothed the top over very gently and turned round and waved to me with a broad grin on this face.

Quite a number of people had come along for medicine, so Daudi and I proceeded to deal with them. Some had coughs and colds, others had ulcers, and there were some men needing cataract operations which we would do later on at the hospital. Then we started to talk to them about God.

'Bwana,' said one old man, 'how can we understand about someone we have never seen?'

'*Kah*,' said I, 'have you ever seen King George?'

'*N'go*,' they replied.

'Well, does that stop you from eating a feast on his birthday, and eating the cow that the chief gave you? Did you say: "I will not eat this feast and partake of this stew because I have never seen King George?"'

'*N'go*,' they said.

'Right,' I said, 'you need to have faith.'

'*Kah*,' said one of the men, 'what is this word, what does it mean, Bwana?'

'It means to have confidence in a person. Believing from what you know about them that they won't let you down.'

Simba was standing behind the group.

'Simba,' I ordered, 'take the boy to whom I gave the medicine this morning. Stand him on the wall there.'

With the help of the African hunter the lad scrambled on to the top of the wall and stood there balanced precariously.

I smiled up at him. 'Between you and me there is a big space now. If you were to jump into my arms and I were to let you fall you would hurt yourself very considerably.'

'*Kah*,' said the boy, 'but, Bwana, you wouldn't do that. You didn't hurt me this morning with the medicine. Your words are true.'

'*Hongo*; if you believe that, you jump.' And jump he did.

I caught him although I nearly went over backwards because he was no small weight.

'*Yah*,' said the boy, when I stood him at last on his feet, 'Bwana, of course, I trusted you.'

'There,' I said to the people, 'that is faith.'

'*Heeh*, Bwana, that's something we can understand.'

Late that afternoon I saw Simba make his last batch of bricks for the day. 'Simba, you have faith in the sun that it will dry these bricks?'

'Of course, Bwana, I know it will. It is the habit of the sun to do these things.'

'Right,' I said; 'have faith in God in the same way, and as we seek to build this town with a place of witness for Him, well, have faith, no matter how hard things are.'

The African nodded. 'Bwana, I wonder what will happen tonight. In very many of those bricks I have planted thorns. They look smooth on the outside, but the inside, *yah!*'

We sat around the fire having our evening meal, and then appeared to go off to bed, but we went into a concealed corner. And from underneath the mosquito-net we had an excellent look-out over the plain towards the spot where Simba's bricks were drying. For perhaps two hours we sat there uncomfortably on our three-legged stools, talking in whispers. The pale light of the moon showed up the mango trees and the orderly rows of bricks. Outside our net mosquitoes hummed ominously, and then silently out of the shadows came a figure, a broad-shouldered small man. Simba thumped my shoulder in the enthusiasm of anticipation. 'Bwana,' he whispered, and then his whole large body shook with silent laughter.

'*Kah*,' whispered Daudi, 'this is the time to watch your step. Look at him!'

With studied thoroughness the witchdoctor started to trample on each brick. We stood, in anticipation of what was going to happen. Suddenly an agonising groan came clearly over the still night air, followed by a piercing shriek, and then the squat figure, moving with truly amazing speed, went across the clearing beyond the well, past the mango trees and disappeared into the shadows that led to the African village, and as he ran came faintly 'eeeeeeeh!' – the alarm cry of the tribe.

Simba gasped with suppressed laughter.

'Bwana, *yeh*, has there ever been such a night as great as this – *Keh!*'

He slapped himself on the chest.

At that moment Perisi appeared. '*Keh*,' she said, 'behold, while you laugh, I have great fear in my heart. You do not know Dawa; he is a man who will strike back.'

10

Sundry Kinds of Death

Early next morning I saw Daudi coming from the village. He grinned. '*Kah*, Bwana, Dawa is limping today. His feet are in sandals, and behold, his anger is very great. I saw him as I went down to obtain a gourd full of milk at the village. When he looked at me, Bwana, his eyes burned like living coals in the fire.'

'Did you get the milk, Daudi?'

'*N'go*, Bwana, they had not yet finished milking the cows. Behold I will bring it up later.'

I turned to where Simba was at work, collecting on the way two crowbars and a sixteen-pound hammer from the back of the car. Among the interested spectators were a crowd of small boys. I recognized them all as patients of mine. A week ago none of those boys would have come near me, but now we were firm friends. The removal of an aching tooth, the dealing with an abscess or ulcer, and the giving of medicine that stopped malaria had produced this change.

'*Kah*, Bwana,' said one of them, 'what are you going to do today?'

'We are going up the hill,' I said, ' to find a big stone, one that we can roll down, and as it rolls perhaps it will break. Behold, we are gong to build a place where medicines can be given, and where people with sicknesses can recover. We will build a hospital that will not get washed away with the rain, for behold, we would build with stones first and put in a foundation that will last.'

Up the hill we trooped. Perhaps two hundred yards up was a large stone weighing several tons.

'*Yah*,' said Simba, 'if this one starts to roll, Bwana, it will go down with great speed, and as it goes it will bump against other stones, and they will break up and much work will be saved.'

We scooped away the loose earth round the bottom of the boulder. Crowbars were put into position, everybody pulled and pushed, many of the small boys lying on their backs and pushing with their feet. It moved a little ... it moved a bit more – Simba's crowbar looked as though it would bend in two – I urged:

'*Mukundugize, mukundugize* – push – push.' The stone moved, everybody pushed, for a second it swung and then rolled down the hill.

'*Hongala!*' yelled Simba, his battle cry.

The stone careered down the hill, crashing into a huge rock. This made bits fly in all directions; on it went and crashed into another boulder. Once again bits of granite, ideal for building, were left behind. Leaping like a wild thing it soared high into the air and landed with a crash almost on the spot where we had planned to build. As we walked triumphantly down the hill, each of us picked up stones and soon we had a pile. Within half an hour the stone for the foundation was ready. The granite boulder that we had dislodged was still too big to use, so we piled round it all sorts of dry grass and thornbush. This was lighted, and soon a very healthy fire was burning round the great lump of grey stone. A kerosene-tin-full of water was carefully poised in the limbs of an umbrella-like thornbush which was above the stone. It was so placed that with the twitching of a string the water cascaded down on the hot stone. There was a series of cracks like rifle fire as the stone broke into a dozen pieces.

'*Yah*,' said the children, 'behold, this is the way of wisdom. Behold, the stone is cracked, and is now ready for the builders.'

'*Heeh*,' I nodded, 'but it's too hot to handle now. Come and let us sit in the shade and I'll tell you a story.

'Behold, in the building of any house that you would have last for any long time, you must have a foundation that is strong, and worth having.'

They nodded their heads.

'Listen, the only foundation upon which you or I or anybody else can build our lives safely is on the

Lord Jesus Christ. Didn't God say "there is no other foundation that we can lay except that one which is laid, the Lord Jesus Christ"? The foundation is the first piece that you build, and let the first thing in your life be the Lord Jesus. Ask Him to be your Bwana, your Lord, and build your life with Him as the One who directs. His Book here' … I held up a New Testament … 'is your guide. As it tells you, so you must build. Here are the words of God's Book. He says there are various ways to build, some as you folk here do, with mud plastered round with sticks, with a roof of grass, and hay, and grass that you pull up.'

'*Heeh*,' said one small boy, 'that is our custom here, but it is a lazy man's way to build.'

'Right,' I said, 'do not build your lives as lazy men. Then there are others who build. They use stones, hard stones like this'… I picked up a piece of granite… 'the roof is of solid metal. It does not rust. This is the building that counts. Be sure that you build like that with your lives, my friends.'

The small boys nodded. Simba said:

'Bwana, that is what I try to do.'

'Right,' I said. 'Well, as you build each day, say to yourself in the words of God's Book, "Be careful how you build."'

I went with him to where the bricks were. Only some ten or eleven had been disturbed by the witchdoctor the night before. Simba grinned – there was a large thorn protruding from one of them.

'*Yah*, Bwana, it is a trap that worked with great guile.'

The whole scene was very peaceful. There was hardly any wind. Overhead soared some eagles, their wings not seeming to move as they flew. The dense blue of the sky was in marked contrast to the brown of the countryside, and the thornbush seemed wilted in the heat haze. Suddenly Simba grabbed me by the arm and pulled me backwards.

'Bwana,' he said, 'look out …!'

Right above me in the dark green leaves of the mango tree I could see a pale green something moving swifly along a limb.

'Bwana, it is a tree snake' – and then in Swahili, '*Sumu sana*, it is poison, very.'

'*Kah*, what a place this is, you never know what's going to happen next.'

'Behold,' said the African, 'if that snake were to bite, Bwana, your days on this earth are finished.'

From the hill above us came the voice of Daudi. '*Chi tayari,* tea is ready.'

We walked thankfully up the hill. Daudi poured some milk from a gourd into the three cups, he and Simba taking twice as much as I did. It was a similar state of affairs with the sugar, and then from a teapot with a broken spout he poured the tea. Simba picked up a large handleless cup and held it to his lips. With a gasp he dropped it and it crashed to the ground.

'*Yah*,' said Daudi, 'what did you do that for?'

'*Heeh*,' said the African, looking shamefacedly to the ground, 'it was hot; did it not bite my mouth?'

'*Yah*,' said Daudi, 'behold, and there is no tea remaining, so there is nothing but water for you.'

I sipped my brew and puckered up my nose. '*Keh*, Daudi, are you sure the water was boiling when you made this tea? It tastes odd somehow.'

'*Neh eh!* Bwana,' nodded the African, 'I did it just right,' and gulped down his cupful of the brew to show his confidence in his competence.

'*Yah*,' said Simba, 'you have a throat of leather to drink tea as hot as that.'

I sipped mine slowly again. '*Kah*, I don't like this. I think Simba had great wisdom when he threw his on the ground.'

'*Hongo*,' said Daudi, '*kah*, Bwana, what's wrong with it?'

'It's bitter somehow; I don't like it.' Saying which I poured what remained of mine over a hardy-looking cactus.

We went down to help with the bricks. I had been at work only about twenty minutes when my mouth seemed to become dry, and pain gripped me just below the belt. Looking up towards the old house I saw Daudi stagger off the veranda and wave weakly to me. I went up to him as quickly as I could, but even as I walked, the pains became more severe. Suddenly it seemed hard to focus, trees looked blurred, and the house seemed enshrouded in mist. I stumbled and would have fallen but for Simba, who had come up behind me.

Daudi was lying groaning in the shade. '*Kah*, Bwana, my mouth is dry, and I have great pain, *kah* …'

The next five minutes defy description, or the description at least would not be very edifying. Slowly I groped my way over to the medicine chest, mixed up two particular drugs in a glass, handed half the concoction to my African friend and swallowed the rest myself.

'Daudi,' I gasped the words with difficulty, 'there is no doubt about it, we've been poisoned.'

11

The Adversary and the Flood

I lay back on the untidy pile of blankets and groaned. Farther over in the room Daudi lay on his side. He looked the picture of misery with all vocal accompaniments.

'*Kah*, Bwana,' he groaned, 'I feel sick. Behold, do you think there was enough poison in that milk to make us travel on the long journey?'

'*Hongo*, Daudi, I think there might have been if we hadn't had medicine to get rid of it and break its strength.'

My African friend shuddered. '*Kah*, Bwana, I feel miserable. My legs feel as though they were stuffed with grass.'

At that moment Simba appeared at the door. Beside him trotted an incredibly thin dog of the sort that is to be found around every African village.

'Simba,' I said, in a feeble voice, 'grab that dog and hold it for a minute.' This was done. 'Now take a drop of the milk and put it into the dog's eye.'

'*Kah*, Bwana, put milk in the dog's eye? But why?'

'Behold, I think there is poison in the milk, and if it is of the sort that I think it is, behold, it will make a change in the dog's eye, which will do no harm to the dog, but it will show us just what the poison is, and that will help us to treat ourselves and get better.'

Five minutes after the milk had been put into the dog's eye the pupil of the eye started to expand until it looked like a cat's eye at night. The milkless eye was a deep brown, whereas the eye with the drop of milk in it was a tiny brown rim with a large black patch.

'*Yah*, Daudi, behold, he put belladonna into that milk.'

I struggled over to my medicine case, loaded a syringe with the appropriate antidote and injected half into Daudi, and he injected the other half into me. We both lay back quietly on the floor, too utterly weary for words.

Simba hovered round the place seeing if there was anything he could do.

'Bwana,' he said, 'I cannot understand why Perisi has not come up. She said that she would come, perhaps an hour ago. I hope all is well with her.'

'Perhaps she is drawing water, and it takes much time to walk from the well here,' suggested Daudi.

'*Kah*,' said Simba, 'I will boil what water we have and make tea.'

'*Heh* . . . tea without milk, Simba. I'll not drink milk in this village for a long while.'

Simba smiled. '*Hongo*, I have a little tin of condensed milk here, Bwana; there is no poison in that. The wiles of a witchdoctor cannot get through a tin.'

He was building a little fire between three stones and boiling water in a cut-down kerosene tin. I lay on my back and looked at the roof in this ancient house that had once been a prosperous mission station, till the lack of personnel and money had caused the C.M.S. to restrict its work, and this house had fallen into decay. As I lay I could see the rough wood of the ceiling bulging down. White ants had had a busy time and had no doubt enjoyed themselves. I watched two lizards on the roof, walking along, upside down, with the greatest of ease. I watched their throats pulsating, and then suddenly I saw the ceiling bulge a trifle. I thought it was my eyes playing me false, and then to my horror a long brown snake appeared. Its weight was too heavy for the ant-eaten wood, and it crashed down almost on top of Daudi. I yelled, and Simba rushed in. Both Daudi and I were too weak to walk, and I don't know what would have happened if our good friend the African hunter hadn't been on the spot.

He whipped up his spear and in a matter of seconds the snake was transfixed expertly by the weapon.

'*Yah*,' groaned Daudi, falling back on the floor again. 'What a place, Bwana, what a place!'

'*Kah*,' laughed Simba, 'behold, I am used to snakes. Am I not a snake-hunter?'

Quite unconcernedly he went out and finished brewing the tea. We drank very considerably, and then it seemed to me that we must have been sleeping for hours when Simba came rushing in.

'Bwana, I have been down to where Perisi is. The reason that she did not come is that she has great sickness. Behold, she draws up her knees and makes strange sounds. She says there is great pain. Bwana,' he came closer and whispered very confidentially in my ear.

Grabbing his arm I pulled myself to my feet. I felt painfully wobbly. 'Let me go and have a look at her, Simba.'

The African helped me as we went down the rough path from the old house, down through the thornbush of the partly-finished house with its fence of cornstalks. Simba's wife lay on an African bed that he had made for her from rough timber. The mattress was rope, put on criss-cross fashion.

She looked ghastly. 'Bwana,' she said, 'the pains are very bad, and I have great fears.'

Even as she spoke I heard the horrible, high-pitched, cackling laugh from beyond the thornbush, the laugh that I had learned somehow to link up with a dangerous situation.

'*Heh*,' whispered Simba, 'behold, Bwana, it is the old women of the place, those who cast spells.'

Carefully I made my examination. Everything had to be done with the greatest of care; two lives were at stake. Five minutes later I straightened my back and sat with relief on a little stool.

'Simba,' I said, 'there is an answer to this trouble. But it lies in a small bottle fifteen miles away. We must get Perisi to the hospital. We must get the car going at once and drive her there.'

'*Kah*, Bwana,' said the African, 'but you have not strength to drive the car.'

'I think I have, Simba, if all goes well. But you must stay here or these folk will wreck everything. Tell Daudi to be ready to go very soon.'

Five minutes later we were in the car. I was at the wheel and Simba and the usual collection of small boys were industriously pushing the car along the level until it came to a slight downgrade. Then with a yell they pushed with all their might. The car gathered speed, I let in the clutch, and with a splutter the old bus started. Ominously from the hills above came the rumble of thunder. Suddenly the brightness of the sun was blotted out by huge black clouds.

'*Yah*,' said Daudi, 'Bwana, we are getting to a time when storms are very strong and very dangerous, drive fast… '

Two or three miles ahead of us we could see rain falling in a deluge. We drove on. Coming to the place where rain had fallen we found the red road as sticky as buttered glass. The car skidded wildly. It took all the strength that I had to keep her on the road. The African girl in the back lay with her teeth set. All her courage was needed to keep back the groans.

The track opened up before us and then after a long downgrade there was a river with muddy brown water rushing at great speed. I pulled up and looked out. An African woman with a load of wood on her head was just stepping into the water on the far side. It seemed to be only inches deep.

'Bwana,' said Daudi urgently, 'behold, in a little while there will be much water in this river.'

I put the car into low gear and moved slowly across. The water was washing against the wheels.

'Bwana, we are just in time, behold …'

But before he could finish the radiator of the car disappeared three feet down into a deep pool. Someone had dug a well; it was invisible because of the muddy water. We were within ten feet of the far bank, but there seemed no prospect of making it. The engine would not start. I opened the door and stumbled out into the water. My legs were still pitiably weak, and Daudi could barely stand up. I tried to find something with which to anchor the car, but the rope would not reach the nearest tree. Then we heard a cry of alarm from the girl in the back of the car. We looked upstream, and there, swirling down towards us, perhaps a hundred yards away, was a wall of brown water. We had barely time to struggle back and get our patient safely on to the bank before the cascade struck the car, picking it up like a cork and floating it for a moment, and then with a sickly lurch it was turned over and swung round. I saw all sorts of things being carried downstream in the swirling mass of water.

We made Perisi as comfortable as we could underneath a great baobab tree. There was a drawn look on her face and she started to shiver.

'*Heh*, Bwana,' she said, between closed teeth, 'the pains are very bad, very bad.'

I had no means whatsoever of sterlising the water for an injection, so I drew up some of the water from the flooded river, five drops of it to be exact, into a syringe, dissolved morphia, and injected. I saw Daudi put his hand over his eyes . . .

'Bwana,' he said, 'I am too weak to stand. My legs just feel . . . just feel . . .' And with that he sat down. He put his head in his hands. At that moment a gust of wind came howling through the jungle.

'Bwana,' said Perisi, shivering, 'behold, the noise of the wind is like the laugther of the old women.'

From where I sat I could see the river creeping up above the wheels of the car, which were forlornly turning. There was a vague slump as a great piece of driftwood hit the car. My two African friends sitting beside me looked all in, and I personally felt the same.

'Bwana,' said Daudi, 'behold, this is a victory for the devil. Surely we are beaten.'

Then came the words of a verse I had once learned.

'*Hongo*, surely we are in bad trouble, very bad trouble, but do not forget the words of God, did He not say through the words of the prophet, that when the adversary shall come in like a flood' … and we all looked at the tossing mass of water and the derelict car … 'the Spirit of the Lord shall lift up a standard against him.'

'Bwana,' said Perisi, 'these are words of comfort. Behold, men will come in perhaps a day's time with strong ropes to pull the car out of the water. It may be dried out and oiled again – behold, it will travel the road. Bwana, what about me? Are the words of the old women to be true?'

'Perisi,' I said, 'there is one big thing I can tell you. These too are the words of the prophet, he said: "The arm of the Lord is not too short to save, nor his ear too dull to hear."'

And even as I spoke the storm broke. Water came down in veritable torrents, the whole countryside was blotted out – wind shrieked through the trees, and from beside me I heard the groan of the girl in agony. Truly we were travelling through the valley of the shadow.

12
A Helpful Wench

The worst of the storm was over. It had lasted for only ten minutes, but during that time about two inches of rain had fallen. Great drops fell from the leaves of the baobab tree and a solitary paw-paw tree that grew on the bank of the river. Waves of brown water rolled past the spot where we were lying. And our poor old car that was both transport and ambulance lay forlornly on its side in the stream. I could see floating downstream all manner of things that I recognized as having been in the back of the car – things which were of great value to us, and which we would never see again.

Beside me, huddled up on one of the roots of the baobab tree, covered with a wet blanket, was Perisi, her face drawn with agony. It was vitally important that she should be in hospital at the first possible moment, but we were still three miles away and all of us were too sick to think of even attempting to walk for help.

'*Kah*,' said Daudi, 'what will we do? We are up against it. Bwana, there is no one who can help us. No one will travel these roads for many hours because of all the rain.'

But even as he spoke came the sound of a motor engine, and over the crest of the hill a mile away we saw a lorry coming in our direction.

Daudi propped himself up on one elbow. '*Kumbe*, Bwana, surely that is Sulimani, the Indian trader, and he must come this way, it is the only road.'

Perisi looked up. '*Hongo*, Bwana, did we not ask God, and has He not provided a way out?'

We watched the three-ton lorry slipping this way and that, very ably handled by the Indian driver. He reached the river, and then pulled up as he saw us waving.

'*Salaam*,' he said, and then raised his eyebrows, as he saw our poor old car's dilemma. '*Heh*, it will get wet if it stops there, Bwana.'

I grinned, as a particularly large wave submerged the old car. 'Sulimani, I am not worried about the car; we can repair her, but I am worried about Perisi here. She is in great danger, and we must get her to hospital at once.'

'Certainly,' said the Indian. 'At once we will put her in the car. We will drive back to the hospital. There is no trouble in that. And then, Bwana, we can return …' —I had always been rather intrigued with Sulimani's English – '… have I not block and tackle and the strong wench that always goes with me in the car? And with these, we will draw the car to safety.'

I covered my face with my hand so that Sulimani would not see the smile when he spoke of his 'wench'

– a contrivance of his own designing. I went on to correct his English.

'I think you mean 'winch', Sulimani – not 'wench'.'

'Why, surely, Bwana, but are they not both the same thing?' He shrugged his shoulders.

'Well, not exactly,' I said, 'however, let us get back to the hospital as quickly as possible.'

A few minutes later the lorry was skidding back along the road. As we topped the hill I could see the hospital in the distance. Never did its whitewashed

walls look more homely, or the avenue of oleanders look more attractive than when Sulimani drove the lorry with a flourish between them and pulled up outside the hospital gates. The African nurses ran out as we stopped.

'Quickly,' I said. 'Get a bed ready for Perisi and a hot-water bottle. She must be put to bed at once.'

Very opportunely the C.M.S. nurse appeared, and I explained to her what had happened. She had already heard how the old women of the tribe had cast a spell against Perisi, a spell which said that she would never have a child. But when this particular spell had proved to be inaccurate they changed their tune and said that the child would never be safely born, or born alive.

At that particular moment it looked as though their prophecy might well be true, but I knew that in a series of little glass bottles packed away in a cupboard in our hospital was the particular medicine which could save that spell from becoming reality. In a trice the Sister had the whole situation under control. A few moments after the girl was put safely to bed between warm blankets the sharp point of a needle was driven home into her arm and the life-saving medicine was slowly injected.

'Bwana,' asked Perisi in a tired voice, 'what is this medicine?'

'It is a very important and very difficult one to make,' I replied, squirting distilled water through the syringe.

'Bwana, does it cost very much money?'

I nodded. 'Behold, that little bottle would cost the same amount to buy as a sheep.'

I couldn't help thinking as I put away the syringe and the rest of this medicine how intrigued the folk who had given three pounds to the C.M.S. would have been if they had known just what their gift would do in the saving of a life, wiping out the grief from an African mother's heart, and breaking a spell.

Suddenly my head started to whirl and my knees felt as though they would not keep me up.

'What's the matter?' asked the Sister.

'Oh, Daudi and I are a bit off colour. I'm afraid we got hold of some poison somehow, and that, and getting rid of it, has not made us feel particularly well.'

'Bed,' said the Sister decisively, and to bed I thankfully went. Sleep was not going to be hard to find, but before I sought it I picked up the little Book that was beside my bed and turned over the pages. I sought out some verses from the 91st Psalm; they went like this:

'There no evil will befall you, no disaster will come near your tent. For he will command his angels concerning you to guard you in all your ways; they will lift you up in their hands...'

My eyes flew over the pages, and I read again – 'He will call upon me and I will answer him; I will be with him in trouble. I will deliver him and honour him and show him my salvation.'

As I leaned back on the pillow I thanked Almighty God for the absolute truth of His words. Even as I said my thanks sleep came.

With the new morning I found the effects of the witchdoctored poisoned milk had completely disappeared. At the hospital Perisi was very much more comfortable – not quite out of danger perhaps, but the edge had gone off a very dangerous condition. Carefully I gave another injection, and spoke quietly to her.

'Perisi, it is completely important that you should rest, that your mind should be at rest. Let me give you the verse that I read last night – "He will command his angels concerning you to guard you in all your ways." Remember, too, our verse of yesterday: "The arm of the Lord is not too short to save, nor his ear too dull to hear."'

Quietly we prayed together to our Father that He would bring this whole matter to a safe conclusion. Outside the hospital I could hear the tooting of a car horn and I knew that Sulimani was impatient to be on his way to drag the old car out of the river, with what he picturesquely called his 'mud-fighting apparatus.' African men and boys were packed into the back of his truck, and we set off bumpily over the road, which was quite dry now. The river which yesterday was a swirling mass of water was now a wide stretch of wet sand, and the car was buried nearly a foot under this in places. Bottles of medicine, pills and all manner of things were retrieved from as far down as a mile away. There was a great deal of shouting and shoving and the whole group burst into an African cultivation song as hoes were brought into action.

When all the sand was dug away, everyone gave a vast heave, and the car came back on to its four wheels with a bump. Then Sulimani tied a weight on to the front axle, and, with what he still insisted on calling his wench, he dragged the old car over the sand, up the bank and on to the road again. Sparking plugs, ignition and battery were soaking wet. We took off the bonnet and dried her as best we could. We dried out the petrol tank and filtered what petrol remained through an old felt hat, thoughtfully loaned for that purpose by Daudi.

I took Sulimani aside and attempted to pay him for his help, but he waved my money aside. 'Truly, Bwana,' he said, 'your work in this country is a work of great good to many people. Was it not you who came at night to save my wife when she was suffering with malaria? Shall I not, therefore, help you at this moment, just for friendship?'

He shook my hand firmly. 'Bwana, sit in the car and steer it. Behold, the people will drag you home. It will be safer that way. Behold, you will travel almost as fast as you did with that engine!'

We all waved goodbye as the lorry swung away across the hard sand and disappeared in the direction of our nearest hospital. I got into the car. Manpower pushed the old bus up the hill, and then with lurches she rolled slowly down the hill, assisted by the small boys. An hour-and-a-half later we were back at the hospital, and I was met with the encouraging news not only that Perisi was asleep but that her temperature was down and that all her dangerous symptoms had disappeared. At sundown I went to see her again. She was awake and completely comfortable.

'Bwana,' she said, 'as I slept, I dreamed, and behold, as I dreamed I was conscious of the angels' hands protecting. I seemed to see a hand upsetting that gourd of poisoned milk. I saw another hand guiding Simba's spear when the snake fell from the roof. I could see the angel, too, when we were in the flood and under the tree in the storm. Bwana, when I woke I knew that it was not merely a dream.'

13

Tactics

Sechelela turned off the primus while I put syringe and needles back into their container.

The old African nurse lifted one eyebrow questioningly.

'Let us visit Perisi and see if she is fit to return to Makali.'

I nodded, and together we mounted some steps and went into the small ward, where I made a careful examination. Looking into the enquiring eyes of the African girl I said: 'All's well, Perisi.'

She smiled and opened her mouth to say something, but before a syllable was sounded a harsh laugh came from just outside under the pepper trees.

'*Hongo*,' came a cracked voice, 'the Bwana has stopped my pain. *Ijego*, the tooth is no more, but that is a small work.'

A younger voice replied: '*Kah! Mudala*, old lady, the Bwana is a stranger to our customs, but his medicines are good.'

'*Hongo*,' said the old woman, 'that may be in some small things like teeth, but in the things of women his medicines have no strength. Behold, he makes medicines for Perisi, wife of Simba, but it will be as useless as water.'

'*Kumbe*,' came the younger woman's voice, 'but why?'

'Did she not refuse to wear round her neck the charm that would protect her from the medicine that the witchdoctor, Dawa, has made, and does she not merely trust in the words of the *Mzungu*, the white man?' Then old Majimbi peered round, and seeing nobody, she spat.

Perisi tapped me on the shoulder and smiled, and in a whisper she said: 'Rather do I not trust in the words of Almighty God?'

I held up a finger as Majimbi again spoke. 'Have not you, my daughter, followed my words rather than the Bwana's, these days before your baby will be born? Have you not charms round your ankles and round your waist?'

'*Ngheeh*,' answered the voice of Nhoto, 'but what of the medicine you have placed along the path that Perisi will tread?'

Again came the ugly cackle of laughter. 'Her child shall be no person, it shall die and be regarded as nothing but rubbish. She shall have shame and sorrow and be the scorn of the women of the tribe.'

There was a bitter vindictiveness in the old woman's words. I looked down at Perisi. She shivered a little and then smiled. Turning to me she whispered: 'Bwana, do not our men in their tribal fighting guard themselves with a shield?'

I nodded.

'Well, Bwana, I, too, will use the shield that God provides, the shield which is called "faith." I will trust Him to protect me and my child.'

'He will do that, Perisi. Do not forget that Majimbi chooses to forget her medicine that was to make you childless. Since this has failed does she not save her face by making another?'

The African girl nodded.

The sun was setting, and Perisi pointed to the blaze of colour. 'Bwana, do not Simba and I pray for each other when there is colour in the clouds and does God not listen to our words and answer them?'

'When we pray, Perisi, behold, power becomes ours. Just as a small match will light a great fire, so our prayers will do great things.'

There came a shuffling noise, and then the sound of tearing of wire gauze. We moved to the door of the next ward and saw a wrinkled black arm come through the gap that had been made with a knife. It grasped a folded blanket, and with no little difficulty began dragging it through the window.

A roll of native rope used for bed mattresses was on a table. I whipped up a piece and in a trice I had put a twist round the wrist, and knotted it firmly and tied it to a bed leg. From outside came a great commotion, and another hand appeared, the knife slashing wildly. The rope had half-parted when Sechelela gave the second hand a smart rap with the edge of an enamel dish.

'*Ya...Ya...gwe, Ya...ya...gwe!*' yelled a voice. Sechelela grinned broadly and picked up a pencil, and in a loud voice said: 'Bwana, get a glowing stick from the fire, and touch that hand with it so that we may brand the owner and know who it is.'

'*Ya, Ya, Ya, Ya, Ya,*' screamed the voice. We grinned. Suddenly the rope parted and we scrambled to the window in time to see old Majimbi roll head over heels, scramble to her feet, and run for the hospital gate at an amazing speed.

'*Kah,*' said Sechelela, 'that's gratitude, Bwana. You remove her tooth, and with it her pain, and she tries to steal a blanket.'

'*Hongo,*' smiled Perisi, 'but will she not trust in the medicine she wears round her wrist to protect her from being caught?'

'*Kumbe*,' said Sechelela, 'did I not say, Bwana, that it is a very hard thing for a zebra to lose his stripes? Be sure we will hear many things yet from the tongue of this near relative of the witchdoctor.'

Daudi and I were watching a cloud of dust about three or four miles away across the plain.

'*Kah*,' said Daudi, 'Bwana, behold, someone is coming. Perhaps it is Bwana Shamba, the Agricultural Officer.'

'*Heeh*,' I said, 'or perhaps it's Sulimani.'

'*Heh*,' said Daudi, 'if it is Bwana, well, the thing to do is to get him to take Perisi home.'

As he spoke, we could see a large lorry coming over the hill

'*Ah*,' said Daudi, 'it's Sulimani all right.'

I went off to find Perisi, who was sitting in the sun.

'Come,' I said, 'get your things together. Behold, Sulimani the Indian is coming in his lorry, and there will be an opportunity for you to get a ride home.' The girl got to her feet with some difficulty.

'Bwana,' she said, 'it will give me great joy to return to my husband, and to return in health. Behold, did we not have great fears when I came over here? *Kah*, Bwana, but the strength of God has been stronger than the strength of Shaitani, the devil.'

'It always will be, Perisi,' I said, 'if only we do the thing in God's way. Behold, do you get tea that is fit to drink when you pour water that is merely hot into the teapot?'

She shook her head. 'Bwana, the only way to make tea is to have a hot pot and to pour boiling water on to the leaves.'

'Right,' I said, 'and the only way to have God's help is to obey Him fully, and then . . .'

The African girl nodded. 'Bwana, I know. Will I not follow the words of His Book wholeheartedly?' As she spoke she had been tying up her belongings in a piece of coloured cloth. She put this on her head and walked slowly with me to the gate. With a screeching of brakes Sulimani pulled up.

'*Salaam*,' he said, 'have I the opportunity of adding to your convenience today, sir?'

'You have, indeed,' I replied, smiling. 'Sulimani, will you find room in your very valuable car for Perisi? She wants to go back to her village. She is better now, but behold, my friend, if you drive her, you will be careful. She is precious cargo. Do not let your foot find the floor when it is on the top of the pedal marked "accelerator."'

Sulimani smiled. 'Bwana, I will drive with skill, care and great speed, and will present her to her husband in good care and condition.'

Sulimani flashed a smile with his surprisingly white teeth. A minute or two later the big lorry was winding its way over the narrow track towards the blue hills which could be seen in the distance beyond the baobab trees.

'*Heh*,' said Sechelela. 'Bwana, there goes a girl who has great courage and great faith in God.'

'*Hongo*,' said Daudi, 'and because of that her life has great contentment. Does it not say in the Book: "Great peace have they who love your law, and nothing will disturb their peace?"'

He pulled a collection of papers from his pocket, and said: 'Bwana, will you come across to the laboratory?

I want you to look at a lot of slides I have stained this morning – all of them leprosy.'

So the day passed as many days do in our hospital, fighting a winning battle against tropical disease, diagnosing it in the laboratory, preparing medicines for it in the dispensary, going round the wards giving injections, doses of medicine, putting on dressings. Then came two hectic hours in the operating theatre battling for lives, and then late afternoon was spent amongst the babies in the maternity wards.

The place seemed full of babies – all sizes and shapes; the whole ward resounded to the plaintive lament of the newborn. I watched African girls skilfully teaching mothercraft to people of their own tribe; African nurses as skilfully dealing with nursing routine and problems, other nurses taking the full responsibility for ushering normal infants

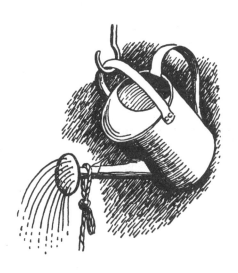

into the world. Then at sundown I went home. What a tremendous comfort it was to enjoy the luxury of a hot shower, even although it consisted only of two gallons of hot water in a watering can suspended from a hook in the roof. A change of clothing, and the usual meal of tough Tanganyikan chicken, and I sat relaxed in an armchair which had once been a packing case, and listened to a mixture of classical music and static from the B.B.C.

I turned down the hurricane lantern and started to doze. In the native village the drums began to beat, and a chorus of throbs seemed to keep time with them. Then I heard the noise of a bicycle bell, and the sound of a brake hurriedly applied. There was a voice at the door.

'Bwana, *hodi, hodi*?'

'*Karibu*,' I replied. '*Nani huyu*, who's that?'

From immediately in front of me came a deep voice.

'*Mimi*, Bwana.'

'Simba!' I stood up, suddenly wide awake. '*Heh*, you Simba, why, what's up? What's happened to Perisi, what's wrong?'

Simba looked at me and rolled his eyes. 'Bwana, I ask you those questions. Behold, Perisi arrived at midday. She was well, she was in my new house. *Kah*, I just finished the roof in time and all is well, Bwana, there is never a house like my house in the whole of the country of Ugogo. Has it not got a solid stone foundation? Are there not places for books? And behold, Bwana, there is light and air in the house. *Yah* …'

'Yes, yes,' I said, 'but why did you come over?'

'Bwana, I received a message brought by a small boy that you wanted me at once. That I must not even stay for food, that I must run very fast. Bwana, it so happened that Mwalimu, the teacher, was coming through the village. I told him of your message and borrowed his bike and came here, Bwana, very fast indeed.'

My mind went back quickly to what Daudi had said in the morning about old Majimbi, that he had heard a rumour that she was up to mischief that boded no good for Perisi. Could it be that it was a plan to get Simba out of the way while the ways of witchcraft were given a little practice?

I put my hand on the African's shoulder. 'Simba, get the bike, come on, we'll put it in the back of the old car. We'll drive to your village as we've never driven before. I sent no message. This is the work of Majimbi and her relation, Dawa, the witchdoctor. Behold, do they not plan some evil? Have they not got you out of the way so that they may perhaps harm Perisi? Hurry and get Samson and Daudi and Sechelela. I will start up the car. This is a matter of speed.'

Simba had gone before the words had left my mouth. Ten minutes later, driving at a speed that was barely safe, we careered between baobab trees, African houses and thornbush. Several Africans on safari hastily hurried out of the track of the fast-moving car. Nobody took any notice as three or four warthogs scrambled grunting out of the way of the Ford as we flew past. Nightbirds flew up as the lights cut a pathway through the darkness. No one spoke a word. We drove without comment through the river where not long before the car had come to grief.

'*Yah,*' said Samson, 'Bwana, the car drives past the place where she had her bath.'

'*Heeh*,' I said, 'and was it not a job to dry her out inside?'

'Bwana,' said Simba, 'drive faster; do not talk.'

I could see his hands clasping and unclasping on the heavy knobbed stick he carried.

'*Heh*,' said Sechelela, 'behold, Bwana, I have fears inside me that there is trouble going on even now.'

Suddenly the old car started to roar like an aeroplane.

'*Heh*,' said Samson, 'the exhaust has fallen off. Pull up, pull up, Bwana.'

'No,' I said, 'mark the place and we'll collect it on the way back.'

'*Heh,*' said Simba, 'that is the thing.'

We roared on through the night. Campfires were to be seen on each side, and then the village appeared before us. We skidded near the side of the marketplace. We went past Sulimani's duka where you could buy anything from spare parts to brown sugar and then up the long hill towards Simba's house. Sharply the road ended, and we leapt out and switched off the engine. In the sudden quietness came a high-pitched cry… *eeeeh*… the African alarm signal.

Simba was running like a hare, even before we had stopped the car.

'Bwana,' he called over his shoulder, 'that was not the voice of Perisi.'

'Daudi,' I ordered, 'you come along slowly with Sechelela; I'll run with Simba.'

We arrived at the house to find the door wide open and Perisi standing by it, a long-handled saucepan in her hand, and tears running down her face.

'*Yah*,' said Simba, 'what has happened?' And then to our relief we saw the tears were those of laughter and not of sorrow.

'*Yah*,' said the girl, 'behold, this last hour has been one of many things happening. Behold, I heard stealthy footsteps outside the house. I heard the noise of an axe, and I was frightened, but Bwana, on my fire...' she pointed with pride to the fireplace that Simba had made her, in the very best fashion, following our own style, 'Bwana, on my fire was a pot of water, the saucepan you gave me. I came quietly to the door and unlatched it.' I looked with interest at the door. It had once been a cement barrel, flattened out and most carefully made... 'and, Bwana, as I unlatched it, there was one who pushed against it. He pushed with strength, Bwana, and did not expect it to give way, but it gave way, and he stumbled in, and, Bwana, as he did so, behold, I threw the hot water all over him. *Kah*, and he screamed, Bwana; this happened not many minutes ago.'

'*Heeh*,' said Simba, 'we heard him. Where is he? Let me get my stick to him.'

'*Yah*,' said Perisi, 'he disappeared through the thornbush with the speed of the *nhwiga*, the giraffe.'

Again her very attractive laugh filled the room. Suddenly a peculiar look came over her face. Old Sechelela, who was beside me, said: 'Bwana, you take Simba and Daudi and Samson outside. *Yah*, it was just as well you brought me.'

We went outside. Simba's face was a picture. 'Bwana,' he said, 'what has happened now?'

As if in answer Sechelela came out. 'Bwana,' she said, 'if you drove over fast, you must drive back faster.'

Simba picked up his wife as if she had been a child and carried her to the car. She was made comfortable once again on an old mattress, and blankets were wrapped round her, and again the headlights sought their way through the blackness of Central Tanganyika at midnight.

I changed gear to negotiate some deep, dry river beds. Sechelela braced herself, fearing a bump, then she spoke.

'Bwana, had it not been for Majimbi's doings we should not have come on this safari, and *yoh!* ...'

Nothing more needed to be said for we all understood that the safety of two lives had been assured by this rushed journey through the tropical night.

'*Kumbe*,' said Perisi, 'God uses the doings of those who fight against Him to make His plans work.'

I nodded, as I noted with relief the lights of the hospital on the hill a mile away.

It was four o'clock in the morning, some three hours after we had arrived at the hospital, that I came quietly out of the maternity ward.

Simba looked up with an anxious face through his cupped hands, but spoke no word.

'My friend,' I said, 'you are the father of a son, perhaps the smallest child ever to be born in this hospital.'

14

Premature

Sechelela was at my door just before daylight.

'Bwana,' she called, 'Bwana … '

A few minutes later I appeared in dressing-gown and slippers.

'*Yah*,' I said, 'how are things, Sech?'

'*Heh*,' she replied, 'Bwana, the child still lives, but whoever heard of a child that size living?'

'Truly, it is a very small one, Sech. I weighed it myself last night, and it weighed just one pound and thirteen ounces. It's going to be an uphill fight, but it's a fight that can be won. You have fed the child in the special way I ordered?'

Sechelela nodded. 'That has been done, but you don't know the other part of the story. Behold, it was only an hour since a baby was born to Nhoto, the daughter of Majimbi, the witchdoctor's relation, the woman who has never followed out any instructions that have come from the hospital, who laughs at the

127

welfare work. Behold, it is eight pounds, and perhaps the best-looking child that I have seen since our hospital was built. *Kah*, Bwana, is she not a woman with a sharp tongue, is not her voice loud in *nyuma ya wachekulu* – the women's ward?

'*Hah*, have I not spoken with force to her when I heard hear say with poison in her voice: "*Hongo*, and where is the one from our tribe who has great wisdom and great learning? Behold, had her learning any value when it came to the birth of her own child? *Heh*, was it wise for her to follow the ways of the Europeans? Was it a thing of wisdom for her to refuse to wear a charm round her neck? *Yeh*, the way of the *waganga* is a better way than hers. Behold, look at my child, and then look at hers, it is nothing but *taka taka*, rubbish. Is there any value in a child that looks like the small monkeys of the forest?"'

'*Kah*,' continued Sech, 'and my words came out very strongly, as the rain comes down the hills after a thunderstorm. She was silent for a moment, but, Bwana, there is a look on her face, a sneer that is cutting deeply into the heart of Perisi. Behold, Bwana, she lies in bed. Her tears are many. Behold, Bwana, her strength grows smaller.'

'I'll be up there in ten minutes, Sech.'

'*Kah*,' said the old woman, 'I will wait for you, Bwana.'

As we walked up a few minutes later she continued the story.

'Bwana, Perisi had very great longings that her child might be a model for the mothers of this part of Africa, to show the people a proper way to bring up a child so that the great sadness of the women of my tribe might be lifted. For behold, do they not see their children die, and die, and die, and die? Do they not wear useless charms round their necks? Do they not bind them round the bodies of their children to protect them from evil spirits? And yet, Bwana, they feed the babies on porridge and they die.'

'*Heeh*,' I said, 'they don't feed them Nature's way – they don't give them boiled water, they leave them lying on the ground to be bitten by ticks, by mosquitoes.'

'*Heeh*,' said Sechelela disgustedly, '*heeh*, and they say it is a spell from the ancestors who had no joy in the child.'

Sechelela gripped my arm almost fiercely. 'Bwana, did not Perisi pray to God for a child who would be a proper child? Did she not fight and struggle and do the right thing? And, behold, see how her prayer is answered.'

There was a hot, angry look in the old woman's eye.

'Sech, would you have anger against God?'

'*Hongo*,' she said, 'I would. Is not God Almighty? Why should He allow this to happen?'

'Sech,' I said, 'keep asking yourself that question, and keep asking it until we reach the place where Perisi is. There is an answer, an answer that will shake you and cause you to feel sorrow in your heart for anger against God. Do you remember the prayer that you and I have so often prayed when we have been in difficulty and trouble, and when the way has not been clear in front? Have we not prayed to God: "Hold up my goings in Your path that my footsteps do not slip"?'

But Sechelela did not seem to be listening. We passed through the gate of the hospital, the children's ward, past the little room where not a year before Perisi's life had seemed to be broken. Together we walked up the steps of the maternity ward. The usual swarm of African mothers were sitting in the sun with their babies in their arms. They eyed us curiously, and then a titter went round the group. I knew that the story was spreading all over the countryside that the Bwana, and what was very much worse, that the Bwana's God, had been *sumad*, overcome by the charms and medicines made by Dawa, the witchdoctor, and by his helper Majimbi. I could see this old crony with some of her companions seated under a baobab tree.

'Bwana,' she cried, 'have you not congratulations for one who is a grandmother? Whose grandchild is a large and very beautiful child?'

'Grandmother,' I said, 'I have great congratulations. *Lusona* to you.'

The old woman chuckled. '*Heeh*, Bwana, and I hear there were other babies born in the night.'

'True,' I replied, 'that always happens at the hospital here in the place where babies live and mothers' lives are saved.'

She laughed, there was a note of high-pitched scorn in her voice, but she made no comment.

Inside the ward lay Perisi, staring sightlessly at a white-washed wall. I went past the bed to the little cot where her baby lay. The very special apparatus necessary for a premature baby unfortunately was not available, but we did our best with makeshift. The child was barely a seven-months baby. It had just one chance of surviving, and that was the unremitting care of its mother. I went across to Perisi and spoke quietly.

'*Lusona*, congratulations.'

The girl turned to me almost fiercely. Her eyes burned in the same way as Sechelela's had.

'*Kah*, Bwana,' she said, 'how can you give me congratulations when, behold, the child will die? Behold, I am the laughing stock of all the women. *Kah*, do they not call my child, my son, *nyani*, monkey?'

Her voice broke down in a sob. For a few moments I kept completely quiet, until she regained her composure. Then I said:

'Perisi, did we not ask God to guide us? Did we not ask Him that this new little life might be of real value to Him?'

Perisi interrupted me. 'Bwana, we did all that, and did you not say that when two people agree when they ask God for things that God does reply?'

'*Heeh*,' I replied, 'truly.'

'Well, Bwana, why has God not replied in this thing that we ask?'

'Ah,' I said, 'that's the point. God's way is not always our way.'

'*Hongo*,' said the girl, running her hand over her forehead in amazement. 'Well, Bwana, why, oh why, has this happened to me?'

'*Hongo*, Perisi, that is a question that I cannot answer. Behold, do you remember the words in the Book of the *Warumi* – the Romans – do they not say: "We know that to those who love God, who are called according to His plan, everything that happens fits into a pattern for good"?'

'*Kah*, Bwana,' said the girl, getting up on her elbow, 'but how can this work out as part of a plan for good? Is not my child so small that it has practically no chance of life? And is not the child of Majimbi's daughter, who followed not at all the ways of wisdom, is it not a large child with strength and good looks?'

'Perisi, you have answered your own question.' I leaned over the bed. 'Listen, is not your child the smallest that has ever been born in the hospital alive?'

She nodded.

'And is not the child of Majimbi's daughter strong and big? It will not be a hard task to look after it.'

Again Perisi nodded.

'Do you not see then that God has entrusted to you the responsibility of a child, who would certainly die if he did not belong to a mother who has special skill and training, special patience, special love in her heart?'

A look of bewilderment came over the girl. I went on.

'Listen, hear the laughter of the old women outside. Do they not call your child rubbish? But if we follow the way of wisdom, the way of knowledge, and look after the child, and feed him in the right way, at the right hours, see that he doesn't eat his porridge till his teeth come, that his water is boiled, and that he is kept in a cot covered from the flies and the mosquitoes and ticks, behold, he will grow and become strong.'

'*Kah*,' said Perisi, a smile breaking on her face. 'I see it, Bwana; it was God's plan to give me the hard way. *Yah,* how hard things have been.'

Eagerly I spoke. 'See, Perisi, it is this way. Now the child of Nhoto is a large well-favoured one, but what will he be like three months hence?'

'*Kah*,' said Perisi, 'poor little thing. His skin will be covered with sores, there will be flies in his eyes, his stomach will protrude because he will be fed on porridge.'

'*Yah, hoh*,' I said, 'and what of your child?'

'*Kah*, Bwana,' she said, 'I will feed him in the ways I have learned. I will bath him every day. I will clothe him in the little garments I have knitted myself. He shall be kept from the *dudus*, the insects.'

'And in three months, Perisi?'

'Bwana, he shall be double his birth-weight.' She pushed aside the blankets, and got to her feet. 'Bwana, I must start on this great job that God has given me, at once.'

I saw her walk over to the cot where the child was. Sechelela tapped my arm.

'Bwana,' she said, 'I did wrong to have anger.'

'Yet,' I replied, 'do not forget, Sech, that God forgives. Behold, He teaches us lessons in this way. Do not question the love of God, rather seek for the purpose He has behind what He does or He allows to happen.'

'*Kah*,' said the old woman, 'behold, Bwana, in seeing that child an old scar was opened in my heart. Did not my first child die, and was not my heart drowned in sorrow? Bwana, it was because of this that I came when I was still a girl to be with those who started the work of C.M.S. Thus it was that I heard of God and learned to follow Him.'

'Sech,' I said, 'cannot you therefore see God's plan? Does not Jesus say that He is the Good Shepherd? And in your own life did He not take your first child for His purpose? Behold, very often does not the Shepherd first take the lambs in his arms so that the mother herself will follow safely to the *ibolulu*, the fold?'

The old woman nodded slowly. '*Kah*, Bwana, I see it now. Behold, Bwana, another scar is healed. *Heh*, very true are the words: "God is love."'

15

Precarious Existence

Together Sechelela and I went into the babies' ward. Carefully I read the thermometer Sechelela held out to me: '98.4^0; normal, good.'

Perisi looked up at me wistfully from the bed. 'Bwana, may I not see my newborn son again. Do they not refuse to bring him to me, and say it is your order that he should be fed through a tube?'

'*Heeh*,' I said, 'it is my order.'

The girl's eyes filled with tears. 'But, Bwana, what is wrong with him? Is his …'

'Perisi – this is the thing. That child weighs one ounce less than two pounds. When he was born I wrapped him up from the top of his head to the end of his heels – it wasn't a very great distance – in cotton wool. About all you could see was the end of his nose poking out. *Heeh*, we had to set to work last night, Mwendwa and I, to make a cot for him. Behold, we have no special cot for premature babies, so did we not get the box in which we keep the small pieces of wood for the chip heater? We tipped the wood all out on to the floor, put a blanket into the bottom as a mattress, and another blanket so that it could be tucked into the box from every angle, and then we wrapped the child up very carefully in the softest pieces of blanket, and laid it very gently on its side, in this box.'

'Bwana,' said Perisi, looking up at me, 'my child is a boy, he is not an "it". Behold, his name shall be Yohanna.'

'Right,' I laughed. 'Well, we placed Yohanna on his side, and then we started the chip heater – filled two great bottles with hot water and put them carefully inside the box so that he would be kept warm, for behold, a baby that size has not the means of controlling his own temperature as you and I have by our breathing and our perspiring and all the rest of it. So we had to keep him properly warm.'

'*Kah*, Bwana, but will he have enough to eat through that small tube? Will he not cry?'

'*Aha, uh*, Perisi, he will not cry, for behold, Yohanna is too small for even that. He must lie very quietly for six hours, and then, behold, I will come and show you how you may feed him.'

From outside the ward came the high-pitched cackle of the old women who were examining the splendid child who had been born to Nhoto.

'*Yah*,' said one old woman, 'behold, has not the child got the ears of his father?'

The baby let out a lusty cry. 'Behold,' said Sechelela, from her point of observation by the door. '*Heh*, I hope the child has not got the tongue of his grandmother, nor yet her thieving ways.'

'*Heh*,' laughed some of the women who had heard the story of how Majimbi, the child's grandmother, had tried to steal blankets from the hospital.

Inside the ward I listened to this conversation and turned to Perisi. 'Listen, I'm going down to my house to read in my book the words of how one should look after a child the size of yours. Behold, this is not a usual thing in my ordinary work, so I will seek food for my memory, so that we may do only the right thing, that the child may live and become strong.'

The African girl nodded. I made my way down to my house and pulled from the bookshelf a book called *Mothercraft*. I drew a piece of paper towards me, and picking up a pencil jotted down the various points. I read for a while and then wrote:

1. Sterile solution of sugar and milk. Then in the corner of the sheet I did a few little calculations working with calories and ounces and the body-weight of the child. Soon I had drawn up a chart of just what amounts of this solution the child should have. I put down the next point:

2. Premature babies cannot suck or swallow and must be fed by a very fine tube. Fortunately I had just such a tube put away for an emergency. I wrote:

3. Watch the child's breathing. It may suddenly stop. Then I noted a string of various things:

    A premature baby is very susceptible to infection, therefore wear a mask and scrub your hands as you would for a surgical operation.

    The child should be moved as little as possible.

    Bed should be changed from side to side every three hours.

The body temperature should be kept at 98.4
and carefully measured.

Then I read instructions as to how a cot should be prepared for premature babies. With a primus stove and a pair of scales I carefully prepared the sugar solution, sterilised it, and proceeded to the hospital with the solution in a bottle in one hand, and the paper with the instructions in the other. I went straight to Perisi. Following the custom of African women she was out of bed sitting in the sun.

'Come,' I said, 'we will go and give Yohanna his feed.'

Three or four nurses came to watch proceedings. It was something entirely new. They were all issued with masks, as was Perisi. I put on a mask and gown and scrubbed my hands. Very carefully I opened the tiny baby's lips, and most gently pushed the tiny tube down his throat.'

'Bwana,' said Perisi, 'how can you be sure that the tube goes into his stomach and not into his lungs?'

'You listen to it, and if you hear breathing noises, then you pull it out, and try again, and then you press just one tiny drop into it when you think it is in the right place. There, now that's the right place. See, I put just one drop of solution in – the child does not cough.'

Very slowly I measured out the solution, and handed it to Perisi, and with a smile that lit up her face she poured it very slowly into the funnel attached to the rubber tube. The nurses giggled; Perisi smiled up at me as the baby made windy noises.

'*Kah*, Bwana, he has had his first feed from his mother!'

I grinned. '*Hongo*, Perisi, you never saw a cow feeding a calf that way! *Heeh*, we must give him just the right amount of fluid. His skin must not become wrinkled up, or he must not show the other signs of not enough fluids within him.'

'Behold, we will watch him with care,' said the African girl. 'Bwana, you tell me the ways.' Then she looked down at the tiny baby.

'*Kah*, my son, behold, you are so small. Have I not fear that you will droop like a flower in the sun?'

The last drops of fluid ran safely into the child. We stood watching. Suddenly there seemed to be a catch in his breathing.

'Quickly,' I said, 'give me the tube.' This time I took care to pass it, not into the stomach, but through the larynx into the child's lungs. I took a breath of air and blew. Oxygen was the thing we needed, but we had no oxygen in our C.M.S. Jungle Hospital, so I did the best I could and blew air from my own lungs. There was a tension in the room which you could almost feel. Perisi's hand was hard on my shoulder – it seemed the child would never breathe again.

'Bwana,' whispered the girl, 'he's gone.' But the words were hardly out of her mouth when the child uttered a sighing sort of breath. We worked for perhaps five minutes, then once again little Yohanna was breathing. Perisi sank back on to a stool, perspiration standing out like beads on her forehead.

'*Kah*, Bwana, I have fear ...'

'Lose it,' I said, 'lose it, because perhaps that will happen again, and if it does, you will know what to do now.'

'*Heeh*, Bwana,' she replied, 'have I not seen you?'

'Pick him up very gently,' I said, 'and just turn him over. Every three hours you will change the side on which he lies. See – tuck in his blankets, make him comfortable. Behold, Simba and I will make him a cot before the moon is much older.'

As I spoke I went to the window. I felt that a breath of fresh air was necessary after that last tense half-hour, and I saw Majimbi, the old grandmother of the splendid new child of Nhoto, skulking round the corner with a pot full of thin native gruel, which I felt sure she was smuggling into the hospital to feed her newest grandchild. I put my head through the window.

'*Yeh*,' I said, 'what have you got there?'

'*Heeh*, Bwana, it is only *wubaga*, gruel.'

'What,' I said, 'do you not know that it is forbidden to bring gruel to the babies' ward? Are not the children here fed Nature's way? Is not milk the food for babies?'

'*Yah*,' replied the old woman, curling her lip, 'what do you know about babies? You, who are a man, a mere man.'

Sechelela's voice came from farther down the veranda.

'*Heeh* … and what do you know about looking after children? Did not seven of your children die, and only one live?'

I smiled and came back towards where Perisi was sitting watching her child.

'Bwana,' she said, 'he's a funny-looking little chap all right. Behold, the cotton wool seems almost to cover him.'

'Perisi, be very careful, your child is not a strong one. He needs the greatest care.'

140

She nodded. 'Bwana, I will give him all the care that a mother can give.' And then, 'Bwana, when can I bath him?'

'*Heh*, it will be many days. Behold, in three days' time you may rub his body with warm oil, but behold, there are many insects, *dudus*, germs, that would get into his body at this stage unless you are very careful. So, Perisi, turn him every three hours. Feed him as I have written on the paper here. Behold, thus he will get strength.'

She nodded. 'Bwana, have I not asked God to give me a child whom I may love, to whom I may teach His way? Behold, did I not ask for a child of strength? I ...'

Taking a New Testament from my pocket I said: 'Listen, these are the words of God. Did He not say: "Ask, and it will be given you; seek, and you will find; knock, and it will be opened to you"?'

She nodded. 'Bwana, I have done that. I have asked God, I have asked Him for His strength. And, Bwana, have I not asked with great strength until I have sweat upon my body? Have I not sought hard as hard, and yet God has given me this small child? Bwana, I had sadness until you explained that here was my opportunity of showing the people the better way with my own child.'

'All this is true, Perisi. Listen, read on what it says in the Book here. Does it not ask a question? See, "What man is there of you, if his son asks for bread, will he give him a stone to eat, or if he asks for fish, give him a snake?"'

'*Kah*,' said Perisi, 'no one would do that, not even Majimbi.'

'Well, listen again,' I said; "And if you men, with sin in your lives, know how to give good gifts to your children, how much more will your Father Who is in heaven, give good things to those who ask Him."'

'*Kah*,' said Perisi, 'I see it. Is not little Yohanna here God's very special answer to my prayer?'

'*Heeh*, and he is given to you, Perisi, because God feels He can trust you.'

There was a quiet smile on the girl's face. She looked at her baby, all wrapped up in cotton wool and tucked cosily into the packing case which was his specialized cot. She had forgotten me, and I could hear the words that she was speaking in an undertone.

'My Father, he is Your gift to me. Help me, oh help me, in the days that are coming.'

As I tiptoed from the room I knew that her prayer would be answered.

16

Fathercraft and Grannycraft

Under an umbrella-like thornbush were at least sixty or seventy women. With them were babies and children and a collection of not-very-well-nourished small dogs. In the shade were set the scales which gave the babies' weight accurately to a quarter-of-an-ounce. All of the women, most of the children, and none of the dogs were listening most attentively to Sechelela as she laid down the law on the proper feeding of a baby. She waved her finger in the air, and with all the tricks of oratory told them:

'You mustn't feed children with porridge until their teeth come.'

I felt a tap on my shoulder, and a whispered voice: 'Bwana, look over there behind the baobab tree roots.'

I followed the direction of Simba's finger, and there was Majimbi.

'*Kah*, Bwana,' said the voice behind me, 'see how her lips curl in scorn. She will not follow the ways of wisdom. Nor will her daughter, and her grandchild. *Yah*, what will happen to him?'

I turned round to see Simba shaking his head in the most lugubrious fashion. '*Kah*, Bwana, if that child lives, behold, it will be *nghani ya kwizina*, a thing of wonder.'

I nodded. 'Also she has small joy or love to us since the chief fined her a cow for trying to steal a blanket. Come on, Simba, we must do some work, you and I. We can't join the Mothercraft Club; come with me, and we'll do some fathercraft.'

'*Yah*,' said the African. 'Fathercraft? Bwana, what is that?'

'That, my friend, is the work that a father may do in looking after his child. Behold, you must do a very special work today. Your child is growing, but it is still so very small that it needs very special care, both from mother and from father.'

'*Heh*, Bwana, but what can I do?'

'Build a *chilili,* a little bed, for the child to sleep in when you take him home. For if he lies on the ground, behold, *dudus* will come and bite him and he may die. Also there is no warmth in the ground and he needs to be wrapped in blankets. Come, and I will show you a sample of how it is done. Take your choice: you may build one with the skill of a carpenter, or go to the jungle and cut sticks and vines, and weave one Gogo fashion.'

A few minutes later I watched Simba measuring in a most professional fashion the various requirements that he would need.

I broke into his thoughts. '*Hongo*, Simba, be careful as you work that you build with strength. The legs of this small bed must not wobble. The child must not be rolled out upon the floor because of the lack of skill or the carelessness of his father.'

'*Heh*,' said Simba, 'Bwana, I will make one with the help of Elisha. It will have very strong legs. Behold, it will stand firmly on the ground, even as do the legs of *nhembo*, the elephant.'

He looked across at me with a smile. 'Bwana, before I go on to my work, may I not once more see the one for whom it is to be built? May I not greet my wife who is the joy of my heart?'

'*Heeh*,' came the voice of Sechelela from behind us, 'behold, I was expecting this. Here ...'

An African nurse with a broad smile on her face thrust into our hands a gown and mask. These we duly put on, and advanced into the ward. There was Perisi, sitting at a little table, herself masked and gowned, feeding her baby in a highly professional manner through a minute rubber tube. She raised her hand.

'Quietly, Bwana, my work is nearly finished.'

Simba looked across at me and raised one eyebrow, whispering, '*Yah*, Bwana, does she not do it with skill?'

I nodded. 'Behold, Simba, there's no doubt about it. Women can do these things in a way that we men cannot.'

He nodded his head vigorously. '*Yah*, Bwana, behold, has she not got hands of kindness and gentleness?'

As he said this Perisi looked up at him, and a look of deepest affection passed between them. With great care the tube was withdrawn, and the baby was placed on his opposite side in the box which was his temporary cot. He was a strange-looking little figure with a cotton wool cap obscuring all but his eyes, nose and mouth. I knew he was wrapped entirely in this warm cotton wool. We carefully tucked the blankets in.

'*Yah*, Bwana, I have joy today. Behold have I not rubbed him very gently with oil? Behold, have I not also weighed him? He has gained three ounces, Bwana, three whole ounces in four days.'

'Three whole ounces,' echoed Simba with a smile. 'Bwana, that is a thing of joy.'

'How much is three ounces, Simba?'

'Bwana, I don't know.'

'*Yah*, it's about the weight of a potato as big as your hand.'

'*Kah*,' said Simba, his face growing visibly longer, 'the child is only growing slowly.'

There was such a drooping at his mouth that I hit him hard between the shoulders and laughed. 'Cheer up!'

'*Kah*, Bwana,' said a high-pitched voice, 'don't make such a noise in here, you will disturb the baby. You men ...'

'Come on, Simba,' I said, 'we'll be getting into trouble. You whiz off and I'll get on with my work. There's enough of that to do.'

The African hunter looked at me and smiled. 'Bwana, may I come to your house, for I need some screws and some small bits of wood, such as you have off the sides of packing cases. This cot will be the best by any father for his child in my country. Behold, there will not be another cot like it in Tanganyika.'

It was again a Thursday; a week had sped since the eventful arrival of Yohanna and Nhembo.

I went to see how Simba's carpentry was progressing. He was very busy with a plane.

'Bwana, with the help of Elisha, before many days this work will be finished. I have need of some screws if —'

Nodding, I led the way to the storeroom where we kept all manner of things that might come in handy some day. What an amazing collection of stuff we had! Nothing was wasted in our hospital. We collected the appropriate material and were just coming out of the door when behind the baobab tree we saw old Majimbi. She was sitting there with her grandchild, who was only a week or so old, propped on her knee. Beside her was a clay pot filled with gruel – grey sticky-looking stuff like paste. The old woman was shovelling this out and pouring it enthusiastically down the baby's throat. The week-old, nine-pounder was doing his very best to resist, coughing and spluttering, but the old woman wiped the sticky gruel from the sides of his mouth and pushed it down his throat with a long and very dirty thumb. Suddenly and rather explosively the child rejected all that had been given to him. The old woman's hand went over his mouth; it was all pushed down again. Open-mouthed, I watched this amazing demonstration of how a baby should not be fed. I was too paralysed to do a thing for a moment, then I stepped forward briskly.

'*Hey*, Majimbi, what do you think you're doing?'

'*Kah*,' she said, 'whose child is it, yours or mine?'

'What profit is there in a dead grandchild?' I countered.

'*Yah*,' she hissed, 'do not cast spells against the child.'

Simba, however, found a soft place in the old woman's armour. '*Yah*,' he said, 'she wants the child to die. She fears that my child will grow stronger than that of her daughter, so she follows the old way. When the child dies, she will say it is a spell. Bwana, you and I know that it is her fear that my child, who is very small, will in a year's time be larger than the child she holds in her arms.'

'*Kah*,' said the old woman, 'your child is nothing but rubbish.' She got to her feet, picked up the pot of gruel, spat, and walked away, swinging the baby on to her back.

Suddenly she turned around.

'*Kah*, Bwana, we will follow our ways, you follow yours.'

She made a clicking noise with her tongue which is perhaps the most insulting thing that an African can do to another. Then again she spat on the ground and walked away muttering.

Simba raised his eyebrows. '*Kah*, Bwana, there is *ikuwo*, fierce anger. Behold, there is an old woman of fierceness. *Oooh*, we will do well to keep out of her way.'

'*Heeh*,' I nodded. 'But the trouble is, Simba, that she thinks that her way is the right way.'

The hunter nodded slowly.

'*Heeh*, Simba, you remember there was once a great king, whose name was Solomon? He wrote many words of wisdom.'

The African nodded. 'Yes, Bwana, I have read of them in the Book of God.'

'Right,' I said. 'Well now, there's one in particular which points clearly to old Majimbi there – just as clearly as the signpost points the way to the hospital. Does it not say, "There is a way that seems right to a man, but in the end it leads to death?"'

Again the African nodded.

'You see,' I went on, 'it is not good enough to follow the way you think is right. Behold, there are those of your tribe who think it is enough if one has pneumonia to rub one's chest with lion's fat. They say this will give him strength to overcome his disease. But what is the end of that way?'

'*Hongo*,' said Simba, 'Bwana, the end of that road is death.'

'Simba, there are those who think that if they wear a charm made from the skin of a white goat they will gain sufficient strength to overcome *mhungo*, malaria.'

'*Kah*, Bwana, that is not the way to deal with that trouble. How well I know it!' Simba rolled his eyes and went through the actions necessary for an injection.

'*Hongo*, Simba, and if these things are true of the way of the health of the body how much more are they true of the way of health of your soul?'

'Bwana, my people have strange ways of trying to quiet the fear of what happens when *mitima*, the soul, when *mwili*, the body, dies. They make offerings to the ancestors, they swallow charms. They wear them too, and build them into roofs. *Kah*, Bwana, do anything, do everything, and still fear remains.

'*Hongo*, Bwana, many drink *wujimbi*, beer, and its fierce relative *nghangala*, mead, that in their glow and the dreams that follow, fear may be forgotten. *Hongo*, Bwana, I know these things. Have I not tried them, and still fear remains to gnaw at you in the times of thought and the times of sleeplessness.'

'But what of the way of God, Simba? His ways are ways of life, surely?'

'*Nghheeh!* Bwana, truly. Do I not know that His is the way that works, even as the ways of health at the hospital mean life and not pain and death?'

'Look, Simba,' I picked up a piece of paper and wrote, 'here is a prescription for you, a medicine that is very strong for soul-health.'

I wrote: 'In all your ways acknowledge Him, and He will show you your path.'

Slowly Simba read, then folded up the paper and put it into his pocket.

Some days later I watched him carrying a very creditable cot to the hospital.

'Bwana, I want an eye-dropper.'

'Has one of the children got bad eyes?'

The African nurse smiled, shaking her head. 'This is for the tiny baby, little Yohanna, Perisi's child. Behold, no longer must we feed him with the tube, we will now be able to use the dropper, and with the mixture that we're giving him now, *heh,* behold he will grow larger quickly. He is able now to swallow, Bwana, and behold, his skin is learning to work like ordinary skin. Behold, we do not need to keep his temperature as we used to. Didn't Perisi have great joy when she found he had learned to sweat?'

I smiled. Only a few days before I had found it rather hard to convince my African staff that premature babies hadn't the natural trick of perspiring like ordinary babies. They have to be very carefully looked after until the skin develops this normal function. From my rather meagre store of supplies I picked out an eye-dropper and gave it to the girl.

'Don't forget to sterilise it,' I said.

Looking at me with complete contempt she said: 'Bwana, do you think I would forget that?'

She was barely out of the door when the African alarm sound came, high-pitched: '*Yeeh! ... Yeeh! ...*' In through the hospital gates rushed Nhoto, the mother of the nine-pound baby, whom we had christened Nhembo, the elephant. She panted up to the door.

'Bwana, quick, help me, my child – please. He has *ndege ndege.*'

The month-old child was convulsing horribly in her arms. In a trice Mwendwa took in the situation and dashed for the hospital kitchen where I knew a kerosene tin full of water was always kept on an open fire ready for such emergencies. I grabbed the African woman's arm and hurried to the children's ward and pulled down a baby's bathtub. Two of the nurses were on the spot in a moment and poured the hot water in. The temperature was quickly adjusted, the African nurse putting in her elbow in the most professional style. Mwendwa lifted the convulsing child from the mother's arms and put him into the water. Every motion was skilful and full of action.

'*Yah*,' said Sechelela, who had come in the door at that moment. 'See, the child has *wubaga*, gruel, around his lips. They have been feeding him and behold, his stomach has refused. That is the reason for his trouble.'

I could see Perisi walking towards the door of the ward and as she came Nhoto screamed at the top of her voice, and pointed an accusing finger.

'Here she comes,' she screamed, 'here she comes, the one who has cast this spell against my child. Keep her away; keep her away.'

'*Yah*,' said Perisi, 'do not talk wild words. Behold, there are no spells cast against your child. The trouble is you followed the wrong way.'

'Who followed what wrong way?' came a harsh voice from just around the corner, and Majimbi, the grandmother appeared.

One of the nurses was carrying out the second stage of the treatment for convulsions. The child was already much quieter and I had measured out a dose of medicine. Once again the narrow tube that we had used for Perisi's child came into use and I slipped it down the baby's throat, pouring the medicine through it. The old woman screamed and rushed towards me, to be met very firmly by Sechelela.

'*Yah*,' said the old nurse, 'what do you do?'

'*Eh*,' screamed the old woman, 'the Bwana is poisoning the child. See what he does – does he not put *cizoka*, the earthworm, down the child's throat?'

'*Kah*,' said Sechelela, 'it is but rubber and a little tube to pass the medicine safely into the child. Behold, he cannot swallow.'

Then, grasping the old medicine woman firmly by the shoulders, Sechelela looked into her eyes. 'Behold,' she said, 'it was you who fed the child on porridge. The Bwana saw you.'

'*Kah*,' said the old woman, glaring back. If looks could kill Sechelela would have fallen dead on the floor at that moment. '*Yah*, do I not follow the ways of our tribe, and who are you to tell me what to do?'

'*Hongo*,' said Sechelela, 'I know the way of helping children. The children in the hospital here live, but hundreds of them would die if they followed the way of our tribe, and you know it. *Kah*, but you prefer to let your mind dwell in darkness, to let your soul dwell in darkness.'

The old woman again made the insulting, clicking sound with her tongue.

'*Kah*,' she said. 'I will travel my own way, whatever you say.'

'Right,' said Sechelela. 'You may go whichever way you like. Behold, look in that tin' – she pointed to the kerosene tin – 'behold, the water is nearly boiling. I cannot stop you putting your head in if you want to, even though I know it's boiling. I can tell you that if you do, you'll burn yourself. I cannot do more than warn you. Again I warn you that if you feed the child on porridge before his teeth come, your grandson will be outgrown by Simba's child over there, the child you said couldn't possibly live, even for a day, and now he is a month old and growing strongly.'

'*Kah*,' said the old woman, clicking her tongue again, 'we will follow our ways, Nhoto and I; you follow your way.'

The nurse was briskly towelling the baby who by this time was normal again. She placed him in a cot and tucked him round with baby clothes.

'*Kah*,' said Mwendwa, 'behold, your words are *chaka*, without wisdom. Behold, the child comes in here a quarter-of-an-hour ago dying, his arms waving, and Nhoto says he had *ndege,* the flutterings of a bird. We follow the way that we have been taught by Bibi and by Bwana. See, the child lives, and is comfortable.' And, as if to underline this, the baby, lying comfortably in the cot, yawned.

'*Yah*,' said Mwendwa, bending over him with a smile on her face, '*yah*, you beautiful thing.' The baby looked up into her face and gurgled.

The old woman, pushing the nurse aside, grabbed the child, tore the blankets from him, wrenched off the little shirt that had been made from a pair of men's socks, and walked out into the sun with him clasped in her arms.

'Nhoto,' I said quietly, 'that is your child. If you want it to die …'

For a moment the girl looked undecided. She looked first at me and then at her mother, shrugged her shoulders and walked slowly out of the ward after the old woman.

'*Yah*,' said Mwendwa, 'truly that child, and what a child it is, will have a very hard time, even if it lives.'

There was the toot of a motor horn outside the gate. I saw our ancient bus loaded up with timber, sheets of corrugated iron, bags of cement and, perched on top of everything, Elisha, the lame carpenter.

'Bwana,' called Samson, 'we are ready to go.'

Two more Thursdays came and went. Yohanna's baby-weight card showed an upward red line. Though still tiny he looked very much a baby to me.

Perisi was getting her things together and putting them in the cot Simba had made. 'Is there not a parting gift I may give Yohanna?' I asked.

The young African mother smiled. 'If I could have a few safety pins, Bwana.'

Producing six of these I solemnly linked five together, and the sixth, with the touch that spoke of long practice, was put to its own special use in the baby realm.

Sulimani's voice came loudly: *'Pande!'*

Perisi with her baby in her arms carefully climbed into the front seat. Simba scrambled up beside Elisha. Many of the staff and patients stood at the gate and waved farewell, as the old car disappeared with a grinding noise in a cloud of dust on the way to the village where we were building our new hospital.

17

The Teeth Come

A month passed, and then came a note from Simba, not printed laboriously, but in a very fair hand in Chigogo.

I translate:

> To the Bwana Doctor,
>
> Greetings to you. Are you well? We are well through the help of God.
>
> We have need of nails for the door; also four kerosene tins.
>
> Yohanna is well, he is fed with wisdom and he grows. This is a thing of wonder to the women.
>
> Also we need medicines to kill white ants.
> Rest in peace,
I am,
Simba

I passed this on to Daudi who laughed. 'It is the letter that the people of our country write; little of news, but, Bwana, that news is good.'

Then came a letter from Sulimani. It was dated ten weeks after Perisi's baby had been born. I quote the parts of it that didn't refer to the price of corrugated iron, kerosene and millet:

We suffer a great deal, my wife and myself, of malaria. We shall soon come for medicine together with injections.

Last year we feel better due to your kind treatment.

Always you shall have whatever services I can humbly render to the Mission.

P.S. A Gogo woman, wife of Masaka the headman in near local village, tells in my *duka* (shop) that the child of Perisi grows with strength. She told her companion he is a real child; they call the matter one of wonder.

I translated this for Sechelela's benefit. She chuckled: 'This will cause many words and many thoughts. Truly many women will change their ways as they watch.'

Perisi's letter came later and was in English.

'There is joy in my heart for Yohanna has strength. He has the health oil. The women come to see our house and have wonder. It is now five months since Yohanna was born.'

Elisha the carpenter came one day with a story to tell of how welfare work was done.

'*Heeh*, Bwana, Perisi is a woman of wisdom. One morning I saw her rake up some of the white wood-ashes from the fire; with water she mixed them into a thick paste and then she swung her baby from her back and rubbed him all over with it. Those who watched said: *"Yah*, she is making the child white."

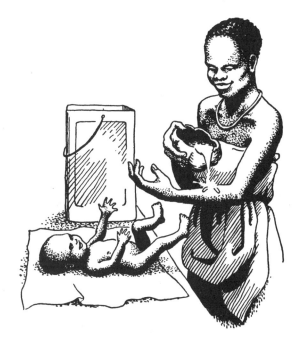

'Perisi looked up at them and smiled.

"Eh," she said, "behold, this is the way to take dirt from a baby's skin. If there is no dirt, then there is no itch. A clean child is contented, and he sleeps, and gains strength. This is the way of wisdom. That is the way in which dirt is taken away, and behold, if there are *dudus* underneath your skin they have no chance because the *dudus* only have joy when there is dirt."

'Then Perisi took a dried pumpkin shell, dipped from the kerosene tin a pint or so of water, and poured some carefully over her arm to see that it was just the right temperature. Then she rinsed baby Yohanna, supporting his back with her hand.' Elisha gave a demonstration. 'The baby laughed and made crowing noises, the mother, too, laughed, and everybody round the place seemed just full of happiness. Once again Perisi rubbed the ashes over her son – carefully behind his ears, and in the various creases, and again she rinsed him.

"*Yah*," she said, "behold, a *chipeyu* of water and the work is done. There is no hard work for any mother who baths her baby that way, and now, behold" … she took a small gourd with a wooden stopper and poured into her hand some clear oil. This she carefully rubbed all over the baby until his skin shone.

"*Yah*," said one of the children, "behold, look at him. Is his skin not *swanu muno muno*, beautifully smooth?"

Elisha adjusted the red fez on his head. '*Hongo*, Bwana, the child spoke the truth. Yohanna is no longer a small baby that looks sickly. *Heeh!* he'll soon have teeth.'

18

Stabbing

There was a most un-African coolness in the evening breeze. Sechelela, who was sitting beside me, said:

'Bwana, stop the car for a moment. It is fortunate that there are blankets in the back. Behold, I would wrap one round me.'

She turned to me. '*Heh*, these are the days when many of our people develop trouble. Do they not get coughs, and many of them the stabbing disease? *Kumbe*, these are the days when Dawa, the witchdoctor, increases the size of his herd as a result of lion fat, which he rubs on the chests of those who have the stabbing disease.'

'*Hongo*,' I said, swerving the car sharply to avoid a baobab tree, 'it's amazing how much lion fat you can get from one sickly goat!'

Sechelela leaned forward and tapped me on the shoulder, smiling, '*Kah*, that is no way to speak of the medicines of the witchdoctor. Behold, has he not very great strength to send away the evil eye?'

'*Hongo*,' I said, raising my eyebrows, 'behold, does it not soothe the chest of a sick man as porridge comforts the stomach of a newborn child?'

Sechelela was still chattering as I drove the car along the stretch of road that Simba had made across the dry river bed and up to his new house. Stopping the car beneath a thornbush we were confronted with a notice written in chalk on the mud-brick walls above a door. It read '*nyumba ya afya ya wadodo*', The Room of Health for Babies.' Inside I caught a glimpse of a model house; a clay pot covered with a piece of

mosquito net, the baby's drinking water, a cot, and the score and one things easily made by an African that mean everything if the baby is to be cared for. On a table contrived from petrol boxes I saw neatly set out a baby weight-card, and one of those intriguing long pencils, blue at one end and red at the other. Perisi was at the door to greet us. Over her shoulder appeared baby Yohanna, looking a very prosperous person indeed. She took Sechelela's hand and then turned to me.

'*Mbukwa*, Bwana.'

'*Mbukwa*,' I replied, '*Za henyu*, what news of your home?'

'*W'swanu du*, all is well,' she replied. 'But behold, Simba has a cough; it only came today; but *heh*, he complains!'

'*Hongo*,' I said and Sechelela smiled, 'and what about the child they called rubbish?'

Perisi laughed and swung the child from the shoulders. He put out his arms to me.

'*Kah*,' said Sechelela, 'he at any rate has no fear of the Bwana, nor doubts as to his skill with babies.'

There was no doubt about it, young Yohanna was certainly a sturdy little person.

'*Yoh*,' I said, 'it's six months since I have seen him; behold, going on safari right through Tanganyika does not give you much chance to visit and to greet.'

Perisi nodded. '*Yah*, Bwana, I just followed out all the ways of the hospital and all the ways of welfare teaching. There was no need of medicine, so I stayed here. See,' pulling the child's lip down gently, 'behold, he is already showing teeth.'

'*Hongo*, it will be time then to make porridge for him before long, Perisi.'

The African girl laughed. Mwendwa, who had taken Perisi's place in the maternity ward, had lifted from the back of the old car a box containing various medicines, a new stock of baby-weight cards, and a pile of bandages. She stopped to make appreciative noises as she held the baby in her arms.

'*Yoh*,' she said, '*heh*, truly he is *mwana muswanu*; *heh*, how he smiles.'

'*Hongo*,' I said, as a figure came through the doorway, 'but behold, his father does not smile.'

Simba had no welcoming smile on his face. Rather there was an expression of deep anxiety. I thumped him heartily on the back.

'*Hoh*,' I said, 'O hunter of lions, what is the news these days?'

'Bwana,' he said, his voice coming slowly and haltingly, 'I am hunted, behold ...' and he coughed, short sharp coughs, his hand going to his chest, 'behold, there is pain when I breathe, there is great pain when I cough, and when you hit me ... *heh*... Bwana, it hurt – just there.' His hand was placed tenderly over the region of his fifth rib.

I sat him down on a three-legged stool, took out my stethoscope, but before I even put it on his chest, his skin seemed literally on fire, and as I listened with what he was pleased to call my *cihulicizizo*, I heard the sound that you can produce by rubbing your fingers together, hard, close to your face.

'*Hongo*,' I said, and Perisi looked at me with a question in her eyes, 'he has got pleurisy, a stabbing disease in very truth, is it not, Simba?'

Dolefully he nodded his head. 'Nasty business,' I said, 'it kills people off by the score.' I saw anxiety flash into the girl's eyes, and I went on … 'Until we had first the sulpha pills and, later, the medicine pencillin.' The shadow of a smile came across Simba's face.

'*Yoh*, Bwana, behold, I suppose this means that you will have the joy of sticking sharp needles into me.'

'*Uh, uh*,' I laughed, 'we keep all the blunt ones for you, Simba.'

I turned to Sechelela: 'Behold, it would seem to me that the way of wisdom is for you and Mwendwa to stay here, and look after things, and for Perisi to come with me to Mvumi. Simba will be in hospital for perhaps a week; she can carry on Mwendwa's work, that she knows very well, and at the same time she can see that I do not stick the needles too far or too often into her poor, sick husband.'

Sechelela laughed. '*Heh, heee* … Bwana, we will do these things. But, *yoh*, I cannot laugh when I think of the stabbing disease; too many of the folk in our tribe have died because of it; too many of the folk still follow the ways of the witchdoctor with his sharpened hedge-hog's quill and with his lion's fat ointment.'

Simba nodded. 'Behold, these are true words, and did I not hear today that Dawa, the witchdoctor, has the stabbing disease as well?'

'*Huh*,' I said, 'I have no joy in hearing that. Behold, I will write a letter, perhaps we can help him too.'

Simba raised his eyebrows, as I took a piece of paper, and wrote in the local language –

Ku Dawa – Muganga ya Ugogo – To Dawa, Witchdoctor of the Gogo country. O great one…

Greetings. I am well, I hope you are well, but I hear news that you have the stabbing disease. A new and very strong medicine has come to our hospital for this trouble. One stab from a needle on three days and behold, the trouble is beaten. I have with me in the village of Makali the motor car, should you wish to return with us, that your trouble may be dealt with, while it is still small. May you rest in peace.

I signed my name, folded the paper, put it into a split stick, and gave it too a small boy with instructions to deliver it to Dawa.

Perisi had gathered her things together, including the cot for the baby and a bundle of all sorts of things tied up in brightly printed cotton material. Simba was wrapped in a blanket and put comfortably in the back seat of the car. We waved goodbye to Sechelela and Mwendwa and drove carefully through the village, stopping outside the witchdoctor's house. A hyena gave an eerie howl as I stopped. The stars shone down from a clear sky, and a fire burned brightly inside the house.

'*Hodi*?' I called, but there was no answering voice to bid me come in. An African woman came to the door and said, in a harsh voice:

'*Yakulema*, he refuses.'

'*Viswanu*, all right, but should he care to taste the medicines of the hospital we will be happy . . .'

She interrupted.

'We follow our own way, the custom of our tribe. You follow yours,' and she turned on her heel.

As I got back into the car Perisi said: '*Hongo*, Bwana, that is their way, the way that leads to death.'

We drove on in silence for a while until before us loomed the dry bed of the river.

'*Hongo*,' I said, as I dropped into low gear, 'behold, Perisi, you remember our journey across this river?'

'*Heh*,' she said, 'will I ever forget it, Bwana? And lying under that tree there –' she pointed with her chin, as we swung out of the sand on to the road again. Then she pointed with her chin towards the vague outline of a hill.

'Nor will I ever forget that bit of country, Bwana. It was there that I was born; it was there, Bwana, that I first put my feet on the road that leads to life.'

'*Hongo*,' I said, 'tell me about it.'

'Among my relations one had died. Behold, Bwana, as I saw them that night round the campfire, my heart was full of the fear of death. I wrapped my blanket round my head, but still there was fear, Bwana, great fear, and then I seemed to hear in my ear the words that I had heard at school.' The lights of the C.M.S. Girls' School twinkled before us on the hill, and pointing to them, she went on: 'Bwana, the words came into my heart, they were the words of Jesus Himself. Did He not say: "I am the way, the truth, and the life, no one comes to the Father except through me"? Bwana, as I lay there in the dark I spoke to Him and I said: "O Great One, I would come to the Father, will you not lead me?" Behold, I knew in my heart that He would answer. So it was, Bwana, I went His way, and as I went I read His Book, and then, behold, some words stuck in my mind; they were these, Bwana: "Truly, truly, he that hears my words and believes on Him that sent me, has everlasting life." Bwana, as I read those words, I said to him: "O Great One, have I not heard, have I not believed, am I not showing that this is true, because I obey the words of this Book?" *Yoh*, Bwana, then it was gone, that fear, for I knew that I had the Life that goes on and on.'

Beside her I could see Simba with his hand tight on his chest, and then a cough that he had been trying to keep quiet almost exploded.

'*Yoh*, Bwana,' he said, 'truly the stabbing disease; the pain of it.'

Ten minutes later in the hospital, in the bed that he had occupied after his memorable fight with the lion, he lay propped up with pillows stuffed with dried grass. I had a full syringe beside me. Blowing out the bubbles I advanced towards him.

'Truly, O hunter, this is the stabbing disease.'

He set his teeth and closed his eyes, with a sudden quick movement I pushed the shining steel needle through his dark skin and pushed home the plunger – the medicine was on its way to deal with those germs that could so easily have caused his death.

19

Needles and Pins

Simba, the lion hunter, lay in bed, his breath coming fast and with each respiration he gave a peculiar grunt that was very characteristic of pleurisy.

I had given an injection and was swabbing his arm with a little bit of cotton wool when suddenly his eyes opened and his teeth unclenched. 'Go on, Bwana, do it. Have I not been waiting? You know I have no joy in injections, get it over!'

'*Heh*,' I said, 'it is done, the medicine is already there.'

'*Yoh*,' he said, 'I felt nothing.'

'*Kumbe*, I must be careful next time to get one of the blunt needles – one of those with a point like a fish hook. You'll feel that all right.'

There was a smile round his lips, a smile that grew as the days went by. Four days later his temperature was normal, his pain gone, and he was demanding more and more to eat. A sure sign, as I told Perisi, of improvement in the physical condition of the male.

It was a week after we had brought Perisi and Simba to the hospital. There was a long queue of mothers standing with their babies on their backs or in their arms, their baby weight-cards ready for marking.

As a little something out of the ordinary, some twenty of the girls from the C.M.S. boarding school had come to the clinic. Perisi smiled towards them.

'Bwana, they have strong desire to sing lullabies, those of the people of our country.'

I turned to the women. 'Have you any desire to hear the songs of the children?'

There was a nodding of heads and a number of '*Hee heehs*' in agreement.

At a signal from Perisi they sang a lullaby. Very soon the whole group of mothers were swaying in rhythm, and the babies peering over their shoulders were very highly appreciative.

'Come,' I called, 'another one.'

'Bwana,' said Perisi, 'this one they call "Merabi". This is the one I sing to Yohanna at the hour of sunsetting.'

The girls waited for Perisi's nod, and then they sang again.

'*Assante wose muno muno*. Thank you everyone very much,' I smiled.

The girls smiled their thanks and stood watching as Perisi weighed infant after infant, working quickly with her red or blue pencil. Simba, who was up for the first time, had come round to watch his wife at work, and was sitting on the veranda in the shade. Once again the junior nurses were repairing surgical gloves from the theatre. I came along to do my afternoon visitation of the mothers and babies, but Simba said:

'Bwana, sit down here for a moment, I have something to show you.' He produced from an envelope Yohanna's baby weight-card. 'Bwana, look, see down here, right down on the corner is his weight when he was born, see it's gone up and up and up.'

'What happened here?' I asked, pointing to a blue downward mark.

'*Yoh*, Bwana, that was the day when he had malaria, but Perisi gave him quinine in the way that you taught her, and behold, his disease disappeared very quickly, see, it goes up.'

'What happened here?' I asked, pointing to another blue downward mark.

'*Hongo*,' said Simba, 'we never really found out what happened there, but babies do this sort of thing, you know, Bwana.'

His son and heir was crawling on the veranda behind him. Suddenly he picked up a glove, which was well on its way to his mouth. Sima said: '*Yoh*, you must not do that.'

'*Hongo*,' I said loudly, 'babies do that sort of thing, you know, Simba.'

He laughed, but the laugh stopped short as suddenly he said, almost in a whisper: 'Bwana, look who's coming.'

A young woman with a black cloth over her head had come up, and she apparently was a new case, for she was asking for a baby weight-card. I heard Perisi's voice:

'What is your name?'

The girl threw back the black cloth, and there was a gasp right round the courtyard.

'Nhoto!'

She drew herself up and put her baby into Perisi's arms: 'Give him the medicines of the hospital, give him the health oil, give him the medicine that brings strength.'

I moved forward quietly and looked at the baby that we had once called *nhembo*, the elephant, now six months later a very average-looking child, with an obvious enlarged spleen from malaria and a deal of skin disease. His eyes were infected, there were sores round his mouth and around his ankles.

Nhoto turned to me almost defiantly and said: 'Bwana, I have come. Behold, was it not yesterday at sunset that Dawa, the witchdoctor, went to be with his ancestors? Did he not take his own medicine, the medicine of the tribe? But he was overcome by the stabbing disease.' She shrugged her shoulders. 'Behold, he has gone to be with his ancestors.' She looked across at Simba, who had risen to his feet, and was holding his son in his arms. She said, as she pointed towards them:

'Behold, have I not seen the way that medicines work with the child, have I not heard how the medicines worked with Simba?' And then very softly, so that only Perisi and I heard: 'Shall the ways of the old women rob me of my son?'

Perisi made a mark on the baby weight-card and said: 'Never fear, you and I will work together for this child. Your son and mine shall grow together. We will watch the red mark move upward on our cards; we will follow the ways of health, the ways of life.'

The baby-scales and cards had been put away, the mothers with their medicines had gone home. Perisi was making some special gruel for her small son, as I came into the ward.

'Perisi how much did the child of Nhoto weigh?'

She smiled. 'Bwana, the weights of the children, hers and mine, were *sawa sawa*, exactly equal.'

We went down the ward and stopped at the bed near the door, the bed where a few short months before Perisi had (to use her own words) greatly of the sadness when she saw her first-born.

I fumbled with my stethoscope in my pocket and turned to her. 'Perisi, when your baby weighed one pound thirteen ounces and Nhoto's nine pounds, when the women jeered, when the witchdoctor and old Majimbi cast spells, behold, was not your heart full of doubt?'

Perisi smiled and nodded.

'You remember the Words of God I passed on to you?'

'*Heeh*,' she nodded, 'you told me that all things work together for good to those who love God, to those people who are the "called ones" according to His purpose. *Hongo*, Bwana, they were words of truth. *Heh*, I will never doubt God again.'

We went out together on the veranda where Simba sat, surrounded by an amused crowd of nurses. '*Hongo*,' said one, 'O, hunter of lions, do not break the child. Put your hand behind his back. Yes, that way.'

'*Kah*,' said another, 'lay him on the cold concrete, would you? Treat him as you would a sack of groundnuts?'

Simba made no reply. He was concentrating on a square of towelling which he was endeavouring to adjust appropriately round his small son. The nurses rocked with laughter at his inexpert efforts, then one of them called to me.

'Bwana, quickly, Simba will do great damage to the child.'

As I came close I saw Simba clutching vainly at various ends of towel and wielding a large safety pin as though it had been a stabbing spear. I touched him on the shoulder.

'*Hongo*,' I said, 'O hunter of the fierce things of the jungle, you may have skill with a spear but' – with the touch of long experience I got the nappy into position and held out my hand. 'Give that to me, Simba; Jungle Doctor to the rescue again – but this time with a safety pin.'

THE JUNGLE DOCTOR SERIES

CHRISTIAN FOCUS PUBLICATIONS

Christian Focus Christian Heritage CF4K Mentor

Christian Focus Publications publishes books for adults and children under its four main imprints: Christian Focus, CF4K, Mentor and Christian Heritage. Our books reflect that God's word is reliable and Jesus is the way to know him, and live for ever with him.

Our children's publication list includes a Sunday School curriculum that covers pre-school to early teens; puzzle and activity books. We also publish personal and family devotional titles, biographies and inspirational stories that children will love.

If you are looking for quality Bible teaching for children then we have an excellent range of Bible story and age specific theological books.

From pre-school to teenage fiction, we have it covered!

Find us at our web page:
www.christianfocus.com